THE TANGIBLE PAST

THE TANGIBLE PAST

Archaeological Sites in the Greek Islands

Margot P. Demopoulos

EFSTATHIADIS
GROUP

ISBN 960 226 042 4

Photographs by Katherine & Margot Demopoulos

Distributed by:
EFSTATHIADIS GROUP S.A.
Ag. Athanasiou Str. GR. 145 65 Anixi Attikis Tel. 8136871-2
14 Valtetsiou St. GR 106 80 Athens Tel. 3615011
34 Olympou-Diikitiriou St. GR. 546 30 Thessaloniki Tel. 511781

EFSTATHIADIS GROUP
Bookshop: 84, Academias St. Tel. 3637439

With love for
Maria, Nicholas and Katherine

Preface

The uncommon beauty of the Aegean islands is incontestably seductive. Vivid beguiling images assault the senses and linger and recur. The Prussion blue sea, the towns stacked like white sugar cubes sloping down the littoral, the balconies crowded with whitewashed tin cans bursting with red geraniums, the piquant smells of fried baby squid, the bleached unshadowed light. But the beauty of these islands does not end with the quickening rhythms of modern life. There is a deeper more profound dimension in every crumbling stone wall, every unearthed field, every unevenly bitten bay. Everywhere the present is permeated with the past.

As more recent layers of soil are slowly brushed away, the vestiges of early life emerge to be seen and touched and felt. We walk the roads and processional paths designed and built by the Minoans, we delight in the frolicsome frescoes painted over three millenia ago, we peer inside private homes and marvel at the artistry of the multi-colored intricately patterned mosaic floors.

Island visitors often arrive with little thought of exploring archaeological ruins. That activity is more often reserved for the mainland, for Corinth, Tiryns and Argos, for Epidaurus, Myceneae, Delphi and Olympia. The popular appeal of the islands is the ease of the sun-drenched beaches and the freedom of the sea. But the island sites nonetheless irresistibly attract.

After a lazy afternoon of swimming off Black Beach on the southern tip of Thera, my friends and I waved the crowded bus away and walked back toward town. Our appetites were roused with talk of dinner. We laughingly trifled with whether we could make it to Phira by sunset. No one spoke of archaeology. It was just then that we happened upon the entrance to the archaeological site at Akrotiri. The site had just opened for the afternoon and only a few visitors meandered through the town of 1500 B.C. That unforgettable afternoon of unexpected exploration led to subsequent discoveries on other islands and ultimately to the writing of this book. Many equally wondrous sites followed. The gargantuan column that alone survives from the Temple of Hera on Samos, the incomparable stone tablets etched with the first law code at Gortyn, the towering view from the dizzying heights of the Temple of the Lindian Athena at Lindos, and many many more.

My initial plan was to include all major archaeological sites in the Aegean and during the years of gathering material I visited each of them. But as the story of each remarkable site unfolded it was apparent that a few but more complete stories would be more satisfying than a veneer of the collected mass. This, then, is not a survey of all Aegean sites, nor is it a guide book for the sites selected. Rather, it is the story behind these ruins, the story of their discovery and their discoverers and the story of their ancient days of triumph and glory. It is the story of beauty and accomplishment.

The exclusion of a site is not intended to diminish its importance. Indeed some of the most memorable sightings were from places yet unnamed, virgin unexcavated fields where the earth is pregnant with finds and just visible beneath the surface soil are broken bits of ancient pottery. On a day that was occupied with the urgency of catching an island flight back to Athens, and just as the wind died down and the canceled flight was on again, a segment of a mangificent grayish-white column was glimpsed in a blanket of pink anemones right next to a busy airline office in a modern island town. That segment of the fluted column was no less refined, no less miraculous than the more celebrated columns from the Temple of Apollo on Delos.

I am deeply indebted to my many Greek friends and relatives, in particular the extended family of my great uncle Gabriel Zounis, who have made my travels in Greece a constant joy. I am especially thankful to them for their *philotimo* and for first introducing me to the magic of Crete. I also thank Nick and Ted Dupas for that first impromptu trip to Thera after our chance meeting in Iraklion. A very special thank you to Katherine Demopoulos for her untiring assistance and constant support, and to Maria and Nicholas Demopoulos for patiently enduring the lengthy gestation. Finally, my deepest gratitude to Nicholas Gage for his inspiration, encouragement and help.

Los Angeles, California   Margot P. Demopoulos

June 1988

TABLE OF CONTENTS

Chapter   Page

1. Knossos 15

2. Thera 57

3. Gortyn 71

4. Delos 89

5. Samos 123

6. Lindos 151

A generation of men is like a generation of leaves: the wind scatters some leaves upon the ground, while others the burgeoning wood brings forth - and the season of spring comes on. So of men one generation springs forth and another ceases.

HOMER

1
KNOSSOS

Hemingway would disapprove. These young bullfighters never had a fighting chance. With the odds so cruelly against them there was a palpable fatalism to their feat. Unlike the modern matador they did not step in front of the bull, taunting and turning with quick dancelike moves. Instead they leapt onto his horns in a headstand, then double somersaulted on his fiery back into, it was hoped, the outstretched arms of a defenseless assistant standing in wait at the flogging tail. In these games, the goal was not to overcome and kill the bull, for he was sacred. The fight was a venerated ritual and, more likely than not, it was the unenviable bulljumper who was sadly sacrificed.

We know of these Bronze Age bulljumpers from the astonishing frescoes in the Palace of Minos. And we know of the Minoans first from Homer, then from Evans. Odysseus, pretending to be Aithon, brother of King Idomeneus of Crete, tells Penelope of the great island:

> One of the great islands of the world in midsea, in the winedark sea, is Krete: spacious and rich and populous, with ninety cities and a mingling of tongues. Akhaians there are found, along with Kretan hillmen of the old stock, and Kydonians, Dorians in three blood-lines, Pelasgians - and one among their ninety towns is Knossos. Here lived King Minos whom great Zeus received every ninth year in private council - Minos, the father of my father, Deukalion. Two sons Deukalion had: Idomeneus, who went to join the Atreidai before Troy in the beaked ships of war; and then myself, Aithon by name - a stripling next my brother. [1]

---

[1]. Translated by Robert Fitzgerald, The Odyssey of Homer (New York: Doubleday Anchor Books, 1963), p. 359

Sir Arthur Evans unearthed the wondrous Palace of Minos, the prototypal labyrinth. It is an inscrutable maze of over a thousand dark confounding rooms on multiple levels, a puzzle of pathways, sudden obstructions and dog-legged corridors that suddenly turn and run in opposite directions disorienting and frustrating the guest. Some passages abruptly end. Others simply bewilder. No direct routes exist. Without Ariadne's unwound golden thread as a guide, there is no real escape.

The prize for those who emerge is the rectagular twenty thousand square foot Central Court bathed in the searing Cretan sun. This generous open space relieves the oppressive confusion of the labyrinth and restores a buoyancy of spirit and a clarity of vision. The panoramic view is ablaze in the flat white light of the summer sun.

The Palace rests on the spur of a hill in the broad Kairatos Valley. It is bounded on all sides by impressive natural beauty. To the east are the limestone cliffs of Ayios Ellas, to the west the hill of Monasteriko Kefala, to the south the gypsum Hill of Gypsades where the valley imperceptibly narrows then bends through the gorge of Spelia and merges with the fertile interior of the island. To the north are the uneven hills that obscure the sea then undulate to the littoral coast just three miles away. The Kairatos River to the east of the Palace was probably navigible in Minoan Crete. The valley was more verdant then, from the abundant streams and springs, and more thickly wooded with pine, cypress and ilex trees. The chalky porous ridges of rock were more uneven, more sharply defined and intersected with narrow ravines. Time has leveled the peaks and filled the cavities with erosion.

The site of Knossos is just south of Iraklion, the largest city in Crete. Crete is a long reclining island, ample and fertile in the middle and narrower at the ends. Throughout history it has been a crossroads for Europe, Asia and Africa. It is about as far from mainland Greece as it is from the Cyclades, Rhodes and Libya. It is the largest island in the Aegean and the southernmost province in Greece. The climate is temperate, the sun generous and seductive and the soil prolific.

Bust of Sir Arthur Evans at the entrance to the Palace of Minos at Knossos

All lands shape the distinctive character of its people and bountiful Crete produced an elegant race, often described as the first Europeans. This advanced civilization was unearthed in the early twentieth century and continuing discoveries have aroused our admiration. Exuberant frescoes, gargantuan storage jars that took eleven humans to move, aesthetic pottery, ingenious drainage systems, sensuous dress and gracious customs were revealed in the substrata of Knossos. These lively convivial people commanded the seas around them and confidently thrived in open unguarded palaces and homes.

When Arthur Evans strolled through the fields of Knossos in the spring of 1984 before his spade disturbed the long reposing site, he found the place "brilliant with purple white and pinkish anemones and blue iris". At that time little more than legend was known of Bronze Age Crete.

Prior to the excavations it was known that King Minos had been a wise maker of laws, a "companion of mighty Zeus" and an able commander of a vast naval fleet that dominated the Aegean with enviable aplomb. Moreover, Aristotle credited him for being scientific and eminently fair-minded.

It was known too that his wife had given birth to four sons and two daughters and that she had copulated with a white bull and had produced a monstrous creature, half man and half bull, known as the Minotaur or Minos's bull. The Minotaur was kept captive in the labyrinth and fed with the youth of Athens. It was also known that Minos's elder daughter had lost her heart to a courageous but dishonorable Athenian prince.

As the excavations progressed the legends were more carefully examined. Some finds gave new meaning to portions of the legend of Minos. He was certainly renown. He was the son of Zeus and Europa and succeed to the throne because of his mother's union with King Asterios of Crete. Minos married Pasiphae, a daughter of Helios, the sun god. Their first-born son Katreus followed his father to the throne and later became the father-in-law of King Atreus of Mycenae, the father of the epic figures Agamemnon and

Menelaus. Katreus was ultimately killed at the hands of his own son, Althaimenes.

Deukalion, Minos's second son, later assumed power and was the father of Idomeneus who battled alongside the victorious Achaeans against Troy, and Aithon, whom Odysseus impersonated in *The Odyssey.* Glaukos, the third son, clumbsily fell into one of the great honey pots that were dispersed throughout the palace. The court physician Polyeidos resuscitated the boy with his therapeutic snakes, a curative herb and his staff which has become the symbol of the medical profession.

Minos's fourth son Androgeos was well known. During the games on the Greek mainland he took part in international fencing matches and was so severely wounded by Aegeus, the king of Athens, after whom the Aegean Sea is named, that Minos exacted his revenge. Whether Aegeus's blows were accidental or intentional is not known, but Minos nevertheless was incited to arms and demanded a notorious human tribute from Athens. Every seven or nine years, some report annually, fourteen young Athenian teenagers were shipped to Crete in tribute. They were never seen in Athens again. Although their fate is not specifically known it is presumed that they perished in Crete. It is believed that they were trained as the fated bulljumpers who performed for the royal court or, alternatively, that they were offered in sacrifice to the Cretan gods.

One year Theseus, an Athenian prince, chose to travel to Crete with the Athenian tribute. Minos's elder daughter Ariadne fell in love with him. She helped him escape from the labyrinth after he killed the Minotaur to release Athens from the tribute. She gave him a ball of golden thread that he unwound from the entrance of the labyrinth so that he could later grope his way back to the light. Ritsos recalls "Ariadne, her beautiful erotic thread unwinding, guiding him in the stone darkness."

When Theseus fled Crete he took Ariadne with him but ungratefully abandoned her on the island of Naxos. She was later consoled and loved by the god Dionysus. And in a curious twist of fate her

Neolithic ruins found on the west side of the Palace at Knossos

Neolithic layer found under the Palace levels at Knossos

sister Phaedra married Theseus following the death of his first wife. In Crete today southerly winds in late spring can turn violent. The Athenian tradition maintains that this is the time of year when Theseus sailed from Athens to Knossos.

Theseus's voyage home to Athens was cursed because of his dishonorable treatment of Ariadne. He neglected to raise the white sails which his anxious father awaited as the mark of victory. When Aegeus spotted the black sails he assumed Theseus had been killed by the Minotaur. Overwhelmed by the specter of his son's death, he needlessly killed himself.

Theseus's misfortune did not end with the suicide of his father. Later, when he married Phaedra, she fell in love with Hippolytus, his son by his first marriage. When Hippolytus rejected her she vindictively reported to Theseus that his son had made sexual advances. Regrettably, Theseus condemned his son and summoned Poseidon to exact revenge. Poseidon sent a tidal wave in the form of

Massive pits where broken pottery from Minoan religious ceremonies were found

a great white bull which ultimately dragged Hippolytus to his death on the rocks of the shore.

Daedalus designed and built the labyrinth to confine the hybrid Minotaur. This same Daedalus helped Pasiphae couple with the bull. He later fled Crete with wings that he had designed for himself and his son. His flight succeeded. His son Icarus, however, forgot his father's advice and flew too near the sun. His wax and feather wings melted from the sun's inferno. Icarus plunged to his death like a trembling plummeting bird.

This is about all that was known of Knossos when Arthur Evans focused on this place at the end of the nineteenth century. And of the site itself Evans said "there was nothing visible above ground beyond the tumbled remains of a wall above the southern slope." But these legends and the scant classical allusions were suddenly supplemented by the unexpected finds buried beneath layers of rich Cretan soil.

Although Arthur Evans is justly the most celebrated excavator of Knossos, he was not the first. In 1878 an appropriately named Minos Kalokairinos, a Greek businessman from Iraklion, first excavated on the Kefala hill. He discovered the first of the storerooms and uncovered the first glimpse of the enormous storage jars or *pithoi* which still dominate the west wing of the palace. He donated smaller pieces of pottery to European museums, a rare occasion when the finds from Knossos left Crete. He named the site the Palace of Minos.

Heinrich Schliemann, a highly celebrated German amateur archaeologist, who excavated at Troy, Mycenae and Tiryns, worked preliminarily at Knossos. The avaricious Turkish owner, knowing that gold had been found at Mycenae, mistakenly believed that gold would also be found at Knossos. He demanded a higher price than Schliemann was willing to pay at that time.

In 1893 Evans visited Crete for the first time. He went in search of sealstones and of information regarding the prehistoric script etched on them. In Crete he found such seals being worn by the local villagers who called them *galopetres* or milkstones. The Cretan women believed that wearing the stones would fill their breasts with more mother's milk. Evans soon exhausted the supply of such stones that he could buy and became eager to dig for more himself.

"In the absence of abiding monuments", Evans wrote in 1891, "the fact has too generally lost sight of, that throughtout what is now the civilized European area there must once have existed systems of picture-writing such as still survive among the more primitive races of mankind." At that time it was generally accepted that the Mycenaeans had been unacquainted with writing. But in Athens Evans had seen two vases with marks that appeared meaningful to him. Further, he believed he had found even earlier symbols on Mycenaean engraved gems and seals. No other scholar had then taken note of these ancient scratchings.

Evans was extremely myopic. Without his glasses he would hold fine print inches from his eyes and see in sharp detail. In his own peculiar way he studied details on sealstones with nearly microscopic precision. It is unquestionable that this myopic vision enhanced his ability to study the curious scratchings on ancient Cretan artifacts.

In Athens Evans found ancient stones engraved with symbols. He felt certain that they belonged to a hieroglyphic system different from the known Egyptian system. He was told they had come from Crete. He inquired about sealstones at the Berlin Museum and was told that they too had come from Crete and that they were pre-Mycenaean. In England he found a similar stone and learned that it had also come from Crete. Evans theorized that some of the Egyptian reliefs depicting the invaders of the Nile valley might represent Aegean peoples. The excavations at Knossos logically followed.

In 1894 Evans began the process of acquiring the site at Knossos. On March 22, 1894 he wrote in his diary of his predecessor's failed efforts: "Long conversation with Hadjidakis about the excavations of Knossos. Schliemann proposed to dig here. Hadjidakis tried to bargain with the two proprietors and finally got an offer of 60,000 p. Schliemann had offered to go up to 50,000. Hadjidakis wrote what was demanded. Schliemann telegraphed refusal to take the land at any price, as he then apparently had other plans. Later

Schliemann came here with Dorpfeld, saw the Turk who owns the quarter, who told him that the whole site belonged to him. Schliemann thought Hadjidakis had deceived him, and came to agreement with the Turk by which he (the Turk) has to have one third of the finds, etc. Then Schliemann discovered that without the consent of the other proprietor who owned two-thirds he could not dig and the whole thing fell through ..."

The location of the site was well known and Knossos was long believed to be the place where King Minos had once ruled. Ancient walls protruded from the rolling slopes of the Kairatos Valley revealing traces of the tangible past. But the most reliable source was the local villager who periodically found potsherds and bits of decorated stones in the fields of porous rock amid the pink and white anemones.

Additionally, as noted, Kalokairinos had excavated there and Stillman, an American journalist, had started a preliminary dig but was stopped by Turkish officials. And in 1889 Schliemann had written to Evans about Knossos. He boasted that he had "discovered" the site three years earlier and complained that to dig at Knossos he would have to buy the "whole estate". In another letter written by Schliemann to a physician he wrote: "The palace is 55 meters long, 43.30 meters wide, and I am persuaded that I could .... comfortably excavate it in a week with a hundred workmen. But not only 100,000 francs or 80,000 marks, even 40,000 francs or 32,000 marks are too much for me to throw away on labors completed in a week whose results - down to the very last postherd ... would benefit the museum in Herakleion ..." Those labors, estimated by Schliemann to take a week, would take Evans a lifetime and continue to this day by the British School of Archaeology.

Director Joubert of the French Archaeological Institute in Athens also wanted to dig at Knossos at the time Evans first arrived in Crete. Evans wrote in his diary in 1894: "... Then some three years since came Joubert. He executed a contract with the Turk who is brother of proprietor by which he was to be allowed to dig on such and such terms, this contract to be valid for two years. He did

View of the lush countryside surrounding the Palace at Knossos

View of the fertile valley seen by King Minos during the religious processions

not come to terms with the other proprietor, however, and the two years have since passed some time since, without renewing the agreement. The field is apparently clear, though the contract between Joubert and the Turk was somewhat obscurely worded." Evans negotiated quickly, appointed himself representative of the self-formed Cretan Exploration Fund and acquired the site. The one remaining obstacle was Cretan revolt.

Evans was precluded from starting the excavation until 1900 when the island was at last declared an independent state. He began the actual digging on March 23, 1900. No one could have foreseen what would be unearthed. During the second day of digging, remnants of an ancient house emerged, with fragments of frescoes on the walls. Evans was convinced that those fragments predated Mycenaean findings on mainland Greece.

On March 27, 1900 he wrote in his notebook with great excitement regarding the initial discoveries: "The extraordinary phenomenon: nothing Greek - nothing Roman - perhaps one single fragment of late black varnished ware among tens of thousands. Even geometrical fails us - though as *tholoi* found near central road show a flourishing Knossos existed lower down ... its great period goes at least well back to prae-Mycenaean period." One week after the dig had begun he found the objects that had inspired him to dig in Crete, curious clay tablets with unknown ancient markings.

On April 5, 1900 he wrote: "A great day! Early in the morning the gradual surface uncovering of the corridor to left of 'Megaron' near its south end revealed two large pieces of Mycenaean fresco ... One represents the head and forehead, the other the waist and part of the skirt of a female figure holding in her hands a long Mycenaean 'rhyton' or high funnel shaped cup ... The figure was life size, the flesh the color of a deep reddish hue like that of figures on Etruscan tombs and the keftiu of Egyptian paintings. The profile of the face was of a noble type: full lips, the lower showing a slight peculiarity of curve below. The eye was dark and slightly almond shaped. In front of the ear is a kind of ornament and a necklace and bracelet are visible. The arms are beautifully modelled. The waist is of the smallest ... It is far and away the most remarkable human figure of the Mycenaean Age that has yet come to light." This figure is known as the Cupbearer and is now believed to be male.

Evans was amused by the Greek who stood guard that night at the fresco. He noted with apparent pleasure: "At night Manoli set to watch fresco, believed by him to be Saint with halo. His troubled dreams. Saint wrathful. Wakes and hears lowing and neighing. Something about, but of ghostly kind. *Fantazi*. It spooks!"

A series of discoveries rapidly followed. On April 15, 1900 Evans wrote proudly to his father: "The great discovery is whole deposits, entire or fragmentary, of clay tablets analogous to the Babylonian but with inscriptions in the prehistoric script of Crete. I must have about seven hundred pieces by now. It is extremely satisfactory, and it is what I came to Crete seven years ago to find ... These inscriptions engraved on wet clay are evidently the work of practical scribes, and there are also many figures no doubt representing nu-

The cypress grove at the perimeter of the Palace grounds at Knossos

The imposing Palace facade at Knossos

The triangular processional paths on the west side of the Palace at Knossos

merals. A certain number of characters are pictographic showing what the subjects of the document was. Thus in one chamber occurred a series with chariots and horses' heads on them, others show vases ..."

When the fresco fragments were found Evans sent for Gilliéron, a Swiss artist in Athens who was reputed to have a highly skilled technique and considerable experience with replicas. Together with Evans he worked on the fresco fragments.

At the end of the season in 1903 virtually the entire palace had been uncovered and work had begun on the appurtenant structures. The discoveries from these fields captured Arthur Evans from the age of forty-two when he first went to Crete, to his death in 1941 at the age of ninety. Knossos was his passion. His active years of excavation continued to 1931 with an interruption for the First World War. During those prolific years he published four volumes entitled *The Palace of Minos at Knossos*. Despite these achieve-

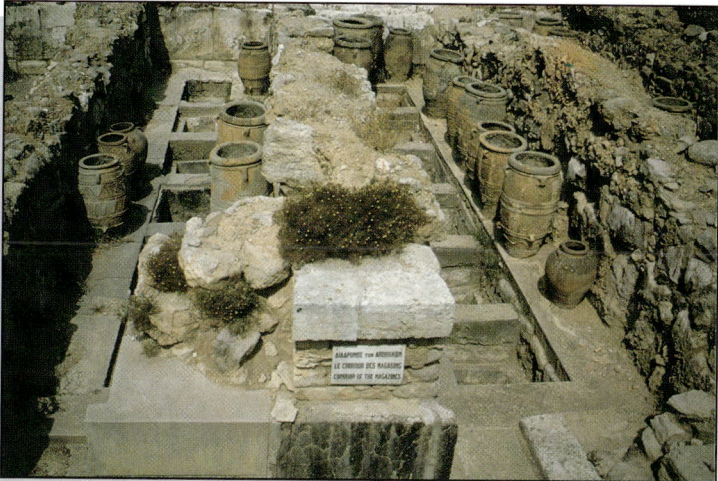

The excavated magazines

ments, however, Evans was plagued with one major disappointment. He was never able to decipher the ancient hieroglyphic script
that first led him to Crete. The early Linear A has not yet been deciphered and the later Linear B was decoded by Michael Ventris in
1952.

From the outset Evans decided that it was essential to preserve
the precious finds and he proceeded to restore portions of the structure with the use of reinforced cement. Wooden frames, initially
painted yellow, were also used in the restoration. The wood has
since been refinished in a shade which simulates natural wood.

For some, Knossos is a disappointment. Evans's recreation of
the palace destroys some measure of antiquity and restricts our
freedom to explore our vision of that world. We are not free like
Manoli, who stood guard at the Cupbearer the first night it was
found, to pursue our own dreams. Everywhere we are confronted
with Evans's determined view.

Despite the criticism of Evans's method of restoring the palace
with materials unknown in the Bronze Age, despite the challenges
to his conclusions, Evans remains highly respected. He is admired
for his perseverance, his unfaltering commitment and scholarship
and his courage to seriously imagine. Prior to his excavations the
world of Minoan Crete was only dimly reflected in Greek mythology and it is thus to him that we owe our current knowledge of their
entrancing world.

The excavations at Knossos revealed the remains of two palaces,
one over the other, one grander and later than the other, both built
upon a primordial Neolithic settlement. Layer upon layer preserved itself through the millenniums.

Under the West Court of the existing palace site Evans penetrated to a depth of approximately thirty-eight feet and discovered that the bottom twenty-four feet represented a primitive
Neolithic colony which is now regarded as one of the largest and
most significant in Europe or the Near East. This level was identified by the crude plain pottery which was dated around 6100 B.C.
Although caves were still used for shelter in this period, rectangular

The Palace storerooms

stone houses were also found with rough pebbled floors. The floor plan, not unlike that of later Minoan palaces, was a grouping of rooms centered around a main one. Hard stone tools and obsidian were found.

By about 3000 B.C. the ruins of successive generations had raised the ground level in some places by about twenty-five feet. It was learned, moreover, that the classical Greeks had avoided the site and so it was shielded from successive generations by a very shallow covering of earth. The Bronze Age of the distant past was remarkably close to the rhythm of modern Cretan life.

In the Neolithic or New Stone Age in Crete, people started cultivating crops and tending animals. There is evidence that the Aegean Neolithic settlers had migrated westward by sea from Asia Minor. Once these settlers learned to raise plants and animals they spent less time hunting, fishing and foraging for food and more time with pleasurable pursuits such as sculpting pottery, weaving

The large pithoi found on the south side of the Palace at Knossos

cloth and constructing boats with which to travel and trade.

Following the use of bone and stone tools, copper was gradually adopted, then bronze, an alloy of copper and tin. The shift from the Neolithic Age to the Bronze Age in the Aegean occurred around 2600 B.C.

What ancient Cretans called themselves or what their contemporaries called them is unknown because no records have been found. Evans called them Minoan after their king and the term has come to denote the Copper and Bronze Ages in Crete.

Evans established three broad divisions of the period based upon the archaeological data and more specifically, the pottery, because no chronological records of any kind were ever found. These divisions are: Early Minoan (2600-2000 B.C.); Middle Minoan (2000-1600 B.C.); and Late Minoan (1600-1125 B.C.). Further, subdivisions were then designated as Early Minoan I, Early Minoan II and Early Minoan III, with similar subdivisions for the Middle and Late periods.

The north entrance to the Palace at Knossos with the relief fresco of the bull on the landing of the control bastion

Another system of classification has since been developed by a Greek professor, N. Platon, based upon the palace periods. He divided the Minoan period into Pre-palace (2600-1900 B.C.); First Palace Period (1900-1700 B.C.); Second Palace Period (1700-1380 B.C.); Post Palace (1380-1100 B.C.) and Sub-Minoan (1100-1000 B. C.). Although many scholars have adopted this system based upon the building phases of the palace and although the dating of the pottery has been modified since Evans's time, most scholars maintain that Evans's system of classification remains the most precise.

The Early Minoan levels at Knossos were identified by copper artifacts, by pottery that had been baked in a kiln and painted and by the presence of bronze tools and weapons. Mottled ware, created by uneven firing, is also indicative of this period. At the end of the Early Minoan period the art of engraving on gems and seals flourished. A lens that was found in a Knossos grave was presumed to be a magnifying glass once used by a Minoan artist in intaglio.

The richest find of this period is an underground vault or hypogaeum which was located under the south portion of the existing palace site. It has provided a wealth of archaeological data. It is twenty-six feet wide and twice as high on the outside, curving up to a beehive vault, with windows at intervals opening into the vault. This and other Minoan vaults suggest the acquisition and protection of precious things and presage the prosperity evident in later palace periods.

The transition in Knossos from Early to Middle Minoan, around 2000 B.C., was defined by the appearance of Kamares ware, pottery so named because it was first discovered in the cave of Kamares in central Crete. It is polychromatic pottery with natural plant designs, spirals and rosettes painted on a shiny black background. The period is also a time when palace centers were first observed, that is, the grouping of structures around more complex centers such as those found at Knossos, Phaistos and Mallia. Around 2000 B.C. there was an apparent shift in power from east Crete to central Crete where these palaces have been found. Simple self-sustaining villages were replaced by consolidated societies in which a few large

The corridor at the North entrance to the Palace at Knossos

centers dominated the land. These centers prospered by trade with each other as well as with other lands. It has been said that increased means and increased leisure are the civilizers of man. The Middle Minoan period bears testimony to this. Increased means and leisure produced elaborate palace centers, sensitive works of art, distinctive dress and graceful refined manners.

Evidence in Knossos of a first palace, which had been damaged by an earthquake around 1700 B.C. was found atop the primary Neolithic ruins. The earthquake reduced the major palace centers of central Crete to ruins. At Knossos this was followed by a much grander palace. The debris of the earlier Minoan settlement was used to make a terrace for the palace. The palace was approached on the west by a ramp and causeways and from the north by an entrance protected by a keep, one of the fortified blocks which made up the first palace. Elaborate drainage systems were built.

From approximately 1700-1380 B.C. Minoan Crete reached its zenith. The rebuilt palaces, designed upon the ruins of those that were destroyed, were much more highly wrought. The cities surrounding the palaces grew and bustled with life. Economic and artistic endeavors blossomed. They discovered the usefulness of metals. They became highly skilled mariners. Their highly distinctive pottery was broadly disseminated. They exchanged goods with Egypt and this trade relationship with an advanced civilization facilitated the early blossoming of Crete.

It is presumed that wealth was established by the barter of objects in trade because the Cretans had no coinage. It is theorized that their ships carried ivory and obsidian as well as skins, olive oil, wine and timber. Ingots of copper have been found. In the absence of evidence to the contrary, it is assumed that these metal slabs weighing sixty pounds or more were used for payments in the balance of trade.

In the second palace period the rural villas of the local governors were the seats of power for the surrounding region and functioned much like the feudal towers of the Middle Ages. In this period more roads were built and the harbors were efficiently utilized as ships re-

Portion of the procession fresco from the South Propylaea as reconstructed by
Evans

A fresco at the Great Propylaea.   *Cup-bearers from the fresco.*

gularly transported and traded Cretan products to the rest of the
civilized world. The new palaces had complex configurations and
were built upon multiple levels. They had stately courtyards, decorated porticos, broad low staircases, narrow processional paths
and a variety of entrances. The royal living quarters consisted of a
suite of rooms that included bathrooms, throne rooms, sitting
rooms and cleverly designed light wells that illuminated portions of
the dark interior with natural sunlight. These new palaces also contained sacred rooms, magazines, crypts and halls for audiences,
banquet and sacred ceremonies. Additionally, there were ancillary
areas such as workshops for crafts and an incoming and outgoing
water system that stunned the modern excavators.

The visible remains at Knossos are those of the reconstructed second palace rebuilt after destruction by an earthquake initially
dated by Evans around 1400 B.C. but now believed to have occurred around 1450 B.C. It is primarily the remains of this second
palace that Evans restored and although he did not always adhere
to the archaeological data, he unquestionably achieved a striking
effect. Evans, using what he learned from the finds, applied his own
inexhaustible imagination and recreated what he perceived was the
true essence of prehistoric Crete. He left in *situ* many skillfully reproduced frescoes originally created by Minoan artists who hur-
riedly dashed paint on wet plaster surfaces to capture the color and
texture of life around them before the plaster was thoroughly dry.
Evans reconstructed many of the cypress wood columns which tapered downward and which had been a part of elevated porticos
and columned halls. He painted them the characteristic Minoan
red, a deep blood red. Evans's work wistfully revived the milieu of
that world, the joie de vivre, and made it accessible and comprehensible to the modern visitor.

Goethe called architecture frozen music or music in space. Evans
rekindled the music of Knossos and its cadence reverberates in the
puzzle of darkened rooms, the wide open courts and the surrounding hills of Crete.

The Palace of Minos is host to busloads of visitors each year. In its time the Palace dominated a thriving city, yet unexcavated, which had a population estimated by Evans to be 82,000. The Palace is an unwieldy squarish configuration, four hundred feet on a side, surrounding an open Central Court. A tour of the Palace without a guide or guidebook is like a walk through Athens in a blindfold. J.D.S. Pendlebury, reputed to have known the Palace about as well as its excavators, has written the most concise and useful guide, a model for many that followed. It makes the labyrinth comprehensible and includes excellent diagrammatic plans of the Palace and its appurtenant structures with the grand tour marked with arrows. A brief sketch of the Palace is noted below, with selected finds and features discussed sequentially, pursuant to Pendlebury's suggested route. This discussion is in no way intended to be inclusive or to be a substitute for a comprehensive Palace guide. It merely illustrates what the modern visitor can expect to see.

Past the kiosks selling replicas of Minoan pottery, over the modern bridge and down a shady wooded path, the bust of Sir Arthur Evans permanently resides near the western facade of the Palace. A familiar first impression of the approach to the Palace is the striking lack of high defensive walls or fortifications. The Minoans were confident in their power, secure with the knowledge that they commanded the seas around them.

The west facade rises above the gradual slope of the West Court in a succession of massive blocks of gypsum that still bear the blackened traces of the fire that ultimately destroyed the Palace. The facade projects outward in irregular segments to accomodate the differing lengths of the magazines or storerooms on the inside of the wall and indicates that the interior plan of the Palace dictated the outer configuration. There are no discernible window or door openings. The gypsum blocks rest upon a projecting foundation of limestone which might once have been stuccoed and painted. Only fragments of the facade have survived but even these remaining gypsum blocks give the Palace from this view a grave ascetic look. Facing the west facade is the stately West Court.

The West Court is distinguished by three deep circular fieldstone pits, known as *kouloures*. The remains of prehistoric homes were found in two of these pits. In Minoan times, these pits were used to contain discarded fragments of pottery that were used in sacred religious ceremonies. The Palace was not only the royal residence of the king and queen and their retinues, but also the official center of the civil administration and of the place of worship or reverence. The West Court is marked with narrow processional ways which are just wide enough for the early Cretans to walk singly, one behind the other, carrying offerings to their deity.

No doorway openings appear on the ground level and no stairways lead to the upper story. As such, access to the Palace from this side is a covered West Porch to the south, off the West Court and in a corner between the main wing and a projecting smaller southwest side wing. The Porch, about forty feet wide, is divided and supported by a central pillar of wood, the base of which is made of gypsum.

South from the West Porch is the state entrance to the Palace, the Corridor of the Procession. It is named after the frescoes that were found here depicting young men and women carrying offerings to a venerated female figure. The skin tones of the young men, as in other Minoan frescoes, were shaded in burnt sienna in contrast to the women whose skin was pale and creamy. The richly decorated Corridor once led to the southwest corner of the Palace, then along the south wall to the Central Court. The Corridor now abruptly ends and entry to the Palace from here is through the impressive South Propylaea. Evans partially restored this area and included a fresco of young men carrying vases in a sacred processional. The most complete remnant of the original fresco is the Cupbearer which is now in the Archaeological Museum in Iraklion. The other figures were modelled on this singular figure, as well as fragments of other figures from nearby frescoes. The young men in the processional fresco are the quintessential Minoan youth. They are seen in profile, in dignified posture, chests forward. Their shoulder-length hair is dark and wavy and they are wasp-waisted and have accentuated their pinched-in waists with decorated bands of metal. Their biceps and wrists carry colorful bracelets. They wear only a kilt, bright and patterned, and drawn to reveal the muscular curve of buttocks and thighs. They each hold a different treasured gift.

The young princely Minoan in the Priest King fresco, found at the opening to the Corridor off the Central Court, resembles the men in the Processional. He is dressed in a more revealing kilt or loincloth, wears a dashing crown of peacock feathers and is leading something that is not visible. He is surrounded by gay stylistic butterflies and walks though a field of tall reeds. Whitehead defined a civilized society as one that possessed the five qualities of truth, beauty, adventure, art and peace. We see these qualities in their legacy of frescoes and we know that here indeed was a society of great civility.

North of the South Propylaea is an open staircase leading to an upper floor that Evans concluded was a Piano Nobile, meaning

The sacred horns

"principle floor" in the tradition of the great Italian medieval palaces. They were great reception halls that were never found on the
ground floor. Evans theorized that in Knossos the Piano Nobile
contained the state apartments and state reception rooms. Scholars
have criticized Evans for constructing this upper story where only
remnants were found, but Evans justified the Piano Nobile from the
findings of column bases and door jambs and the remnants of broken steps.

An open staircase leads to a higher level with a breathtaking view
of the surrounding countryside. An exposed Long Corridor cuts
through the center of the Piano Nobile providing needed sunlight to
the adjacent rooms. At the southern end of the Corridor and down
a wooden staircase is the lower story with more than twenty magazines or windowless storerooms which contained large storage jars
or *pithoi.* These storage rooms contained the oil, wine and grain
that were offered in tribute to King Minos. The storerooms also
contained sunken chests which held more precious possessions,
such as gold foil and inlaid caskets. Kalokairinos had excavated
some of these magazines in 1878. He found thick clay shards that
were expertly reassembled into these massive unmovable jars.

Hieroglyphic tablets were found at the north end of the Long
Corridor. Around the corner a winding ramp passes the place
where the Saffron Gatherer was found. The fresco of The Saffron
Gatherer is a delightful bluish grey figure surrounded by a wild
spray of crocuses. He appears to be picking the flowers for arrange-
ments in baskets and pots which have been placed on the rocks. The
background is the familiar Minoan red. Evans restored the figure as
a boy but the tail that arches above the figure suggests that it may
have been an impish monkey.

Through a door at the bottom of the ramp is the restored North-
west Portico and to the left the Lustral Area where small flasks of
oil were found. It is believed that Minoan visitors anointed or puri-
fied themselves with oil before entering the Palace proper.

To the west and away from the Palace is the open Theatral Area.
It is a small space with two tiers of steps forming a right angle and,

Lower Palace level

The artful Palace doorways as rebuilt by Evans at Knossos

in a corner, an elevated surface which may have been the honored place or dais where Minos sat in review of his troops or in rapt enjoyment of a dance performance or in a receiving line for visiting dignitaries. Although the Theatral Area is too small for a bullring, it may well have been the place to which Homer referred as a "dancing place that in wide Knossos Daedalus wrought for Ariadne of the lovely tresses."

The Theatral Area faces westward to the pathway that is called "the oldest road in Europe." It is a narrow road paved with stone slabs and on either side are wide flat borders and drains. It was once a main thoroughfare to the bustling center of the ancient city.

Leaving the Theatral Area and returning to the Palace from the north side, entry to the Palace is through a narrow portal beside the Northeast Propylaeum and then through a high hall, supported by ten massive square columns, known as the Custom House. Evans believed that this was the port of entry for the goods which were delivered to King Minos and stocked in the Palace storerooms. From here is an ascent to the Central Court and to the North entrance, the most impressive entry to the Palace. Elevated porticos brightly decorated with Minoan red columns and brightly colored frescoes lined both sides of a ramp, approximately twenty meters long, that sloped upward to a higher level of the Central Court. Today only a portion of a portico on one side of the ramp has been rencon-structed along with the powerful and realistic Charging Bull fresco, done in relief.

Atop the ramp is the Central Court with an expansive view of the Cretan landscape. It is bounded by foundation walls in an ordered chessboard pattern. The Central Court is the focal point of the entire Palace complex and contrasts markedly with the dark winding interior. Some have suggested that it was the site of the bullring, but that seems unlikely. The audience would have been unprotected from the blind rage of the taunted bulls.

The Central Court separates the West Wing, where the official rooms and state quarters were located from the East Wing which housed the private domestic suites and the various workshops. The

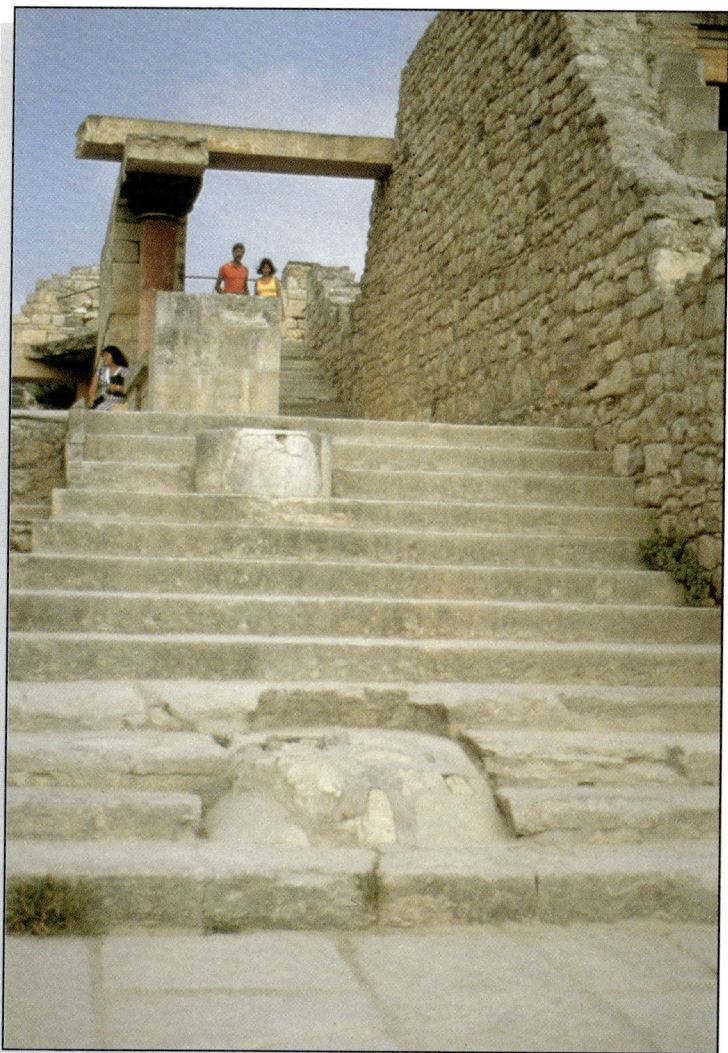

Wide elegant staircase leading to upper level

first suite of rooms west of the Court includes the Throne Room, the most renown room in the Palace, and adjacent royal rooms which were built in the final period before the Palace was destroyed. The Throne Room is marked by a simple, straight-back armless stone throne. The surrounding benches suggest eating for an advisory group or official council or perhaps a court of law. The Throne Room is inaccessible from the interior of the Palace and is reached only through an Anteroom off the Central Court. It receives dim indirect light through the doorways of the Anteroom and a nearby light well. The cool darkness gives the suite of rooms a somber air of mystery.

The Anteroom has stone benches on the north and south walls and a reproduction of the throne in wood. The reproduction has been placed where charred remains were found. The gypsum throne of King Minos remains in the Throne Room precisely where it was found. A copy of his throne was made for the President of the International Court in The Hague because Minos is believed to be the world's first judge.

A sunken area or lustral basin, partially partitioned, was found off the side of the Throne Room. It too was used for purification purposes. It appears that a ritual of purification customarily preceded all official proceedings.

During the excavations Evans discovered the remains of a pair of reclining griffins facing each other on either side of a doorway on the west wall of the Throne Room. On April 19, 1900 Evans wrote: "It now becomes clear that a guardian griffin stood on either side of the door leading to the room beyond the bath chamber. What was it?"

These fragments inspired Evans to paint stylized designs, in bright red, blue and chrome yellow and in elaborate detail, of a similar pair of griffins on the wall behind the actual throne. Some have supposed that the ubiquitous bull rather than the imaginary griffin was more likely the adopted symbol guarding the royal throne. Evans, however, had found a fragment near the throne which suggested the presence of griffin frescoes and he characteri-

The open courtyard

One of the open Palace drains at Knossos

stically followed his own intuition. The spirit of Minos resonates in these rooms where the luminous incongruous frescoes dominate the mystical darkness and where, ironically, his modest throne survived the long millenniums.

Just outside the northeast corner of the Anteroom to the Throne Room is a spiral staircase which leads to the second floor. A series of rooms and a terrace were reconstructed on the second floor to correspond to the rooms below. Reproductions of several frescoes have been placed in a room directly over the Throne Room. The Ladies in Blue fresco, found in the East Wing of the Palace, is reproduced here. Ladies in Blue was partially based on fragments from other frescoes, which enabled the restorers to complete the work with as much verisimilitude as possible. The ladies are drawn in profile, their dark hair arranged in elaborate fashion, bedecked with multiple strands of jewels. The most intriguing feature, however, is the posture of their arms and hands. The arms are bent at the elbow with the hands gesturing upward in an expression of alluring invitation. The background is a clear Mediterranean blue. It seems inconceivable that this life of refinement flourished in Crete a good thousand years before Pericles.

Other frescoes in the same room are the Captain of the Blacks, which portrays a young Minoan soldier leading his troops, and the Saffron Gatherer, noted above. The other remarkable fresco is the Toreador fresco.

The Toreador presents two women and one man in the act of defying the power and ferocity of a bull. One athlete grabs hold of the horns, double somersaults on the back and jumps off the bull while another athlete begins the same feat on the same angry animal before the first one is off the bull's back. The women, as in other frescoes, are colored with pale milky skin. They are bare-breasted, adorned with bracelets, necklaces and jeweled hair ornaments, and dressed in short kilts and footwear that reaches the mid-calf. Are these the youth of Athens, trained to perform this impossible feat for the pleasure of the Cretan audience? Is this indeed the very act of cruel sacred sacrifice?

This room of frescoes and the rooms beyond lead to the exposed Long Corridor, to the left of which is a broad flight of steps leading back down to the Central Court.

On the opposite side of the Central Court is the East Wing which is said to have been of greater architectural and human interest. While the West Wing had two floors atop the ground floor, the more spacious East Wing had four floors above the ground floor with the private quarters of the royal couple two levels below the Central Court.

At about the halfway mark off the Central Court is the still well-preserved and partially reconstructed Grand Staircase, added in the rebuilding of the Palace after 1700 B.C. The Staircase has been hailed as one of the greatest feats of modern architectural restoration. It begins at the Hall of the Colonnades and rises to the second and third floors in broad low alabaster steps, suitable for the processions when the acolytes paid homage to their king.

Lustral basin

The landings of the Staircase were embellished with frescoes. On the east wall of the balcony of the first landing, or Upper Hall of the Colonnades, is a reproduction of an immense Shield fresco. It shows hugh double shields, each in a contour of a figure-of-eight, allowing the warrior to clasp the otherwise unwieldy shield at the axis. The mottled hide of a bull is carefully duplicated and a yellow band down the middle of the shields imitates the bristlelike hair which runs down the center of a bull's back. The shields were made of double thickness in areas where they were most vulnerable to attack. The frescoes include meticulous fascimiles of the stitches used to bind this double thickness.

At the bottom of the Grand Staircase is the entry to the Hall of the Colonnades. An immense light well illuminates the adjacent rooms of several stories with mildly reflected blades of light. This light well not only lit this multi-level space, but also protected the Minoans from the fierce dust and heat of the Cretan summer and the cold biting winds of late spring.

The opening in the northeast corner of the Hall of the Colonnades leads to the Hall of the Double Axes, named for the double ax markings etched in stone at the entry. Evans called this room the King's Megaron or private living quarters. To the left is the Outer Hall of the Double Axes, a rectangular room with partitions which could be separately closed. A spiral fresco was also found here, similar to that of the large Shield fresco, but absent the paintings of shields. It is presumed that the actual ox hide shields hung here. These shields were nearly the height of a grown person and covered with thick heavy ox hide. They must have anchored the warriors who carried them.

An opening in the south wall of the Hall of the Double Axes leads to an angular gypsum-lined corridor which leads to the Queen's Megaron, similar in design to the King's, but on a smaller scale. This dark space is lit by two small light wells and by the presence of fresh natural frescoes. A large Dolphin fresco dominates the entry. A school of blue dolphins, surrounded by smaller blue and pink fish and sea sponges and sea-urchins, glide through the sea, their waving fins making bubbles as they pass. This natural design may have been intended to compensate for the deep cavernous space and the lack of access to the Central Court two levels above or to any outdoor portico.

The Queen's Megaron is divided in half, with a light well on each side and with stone benches surrounding the dividing pillars. One wooden pillar is ornamented with a series of three rectangles, arranged vertically. The top rectangle is a reproduction of a graceful Minoan dancer and the lower two, which might once have been painted as well, have been left blank by the excavators.

West of the Queen's Megaron is the Queen's Bath, approximately seven feet by twelve feet, and considerably restored in plaster. It has a whitish crystalline gypsum floor and an ornamental dado. A paving block was removed in the Bath to expose the earlier phases of the Palace and to illustrate that the East Wing was in a constant state of renovation.

The Queen's Bath is equipped with a small sitting, or more likely standing, earthenware bathtub. The bathtub is just over a yard long, hardly long enough to accomodate a seated woman, legs outstretched. More likely she stood to bathe, with maidservants pouring water over her. The tub's drainage hole has caused considerable consternation because no evidence has been found of drainage provisions on or under the floor. What, however, would be the point of an ineffectual drainage hole? If the drain were opened it would flood the Queen's Bath. Have the excavators missed something, did the destruction of the Palace obscure the drains here or, more probably, was the bathtub moved to one of the Palace drains when the Queen decided to bathe?

An opening south of the Bath and in the southwest corner of the Queen's Megaron leads to the confining Corridor of the Painted Pithos and the infamous Queen's Toilet Room, the subject of much discourse because of the discovery of a flush toilet. It is a small room lit by a single light well. There are holes in the wall which connect with receptacles on an upper level and which led the excavators to conclude that the Queen had the luxury of running water. A toilet with a flush mechanism was found against the east wall along with a corresponding system of drains and sewers and fragments of a wooden toilet seat. The drainage stystem is visible in a recessed area at the beginning of the dark corridor that leads back to the Hall of the Colonnades. The waste was diverted outside the Palace to the east slope where a central drain emptied into the Kairatos River.

At intervals there were minor sewers and manholes for inspection of the system. The underground drains were ventilated by airshafts and made accessible by manholes. Evans said that these underground drains were "so roomy that (his) Cretan workmen spent whole days in them without inconvenience."

The rooms north of the Queen's Megaron were devoted to workshops for potters, stonemasons, lapidaries and others. There were also rooms where furniture was made and repaired. In the north-south corridor of the artisan's quarters, Evans found an elegant gaming board set with crystal and ivory mosaic, with gold settings and silver lining under some of the crystal plaques. On an escarpment to the east, the massive East Wall survives from the first palace when the hillside was cut away for the palace in narrow descending terraces.

Magazines containing the Giant Pithoi, the largest ever found, were also located in the East Wing and were also remnants of the first palace. They are overpowering and are twice as high as a tall person. Evans said that it took eleven men with poles and ropes to move them. They must have been installed first, before the interior Palace walls were erected, then permanently walled in. Although they are too gargantuan to have been moved, they are curiously designed with handles and knobs and a raised rope pattern as if to facilitate easy gripping and handling.

In the Palace itself rainwater was collected from the roofs in the rainy season, then directed to open conduits which traced the steps to the postern entrance. The flow of that rainwater was cleverly controlled. If allowed to flow unchecked in the open channels its speed would have increased down the incline and consequently the water would have spilled over the landings of the stairs at the sharp corners. In an amazing feat of architectural engineering, the water was directed down a progression of small parabolic waterfalls, thereby slowing the water's flow. Evans rightly said that "Nothing in the whole building gives such an impression of the result of long generations of intelligent experience on the part of the Minoan engineers as the parabolic curve of the channels."

Two basins were found near the bottom of the stairs where sediment was allowed to deposit before the clean water continued its flow. Evans called this the Palace laundry. In all there were three separate and distinct water and drainage systems in the Palace, one for drinking water, one for the collection of rainwater and one to channel out the sewage.

The East Bastion, the back door to the Palace, or the little hidden door as some have said, is of curious interest because of its pure utilitarian simplicity. Evans offered that it would have been the least inviting entrance because of the maleodorous outlets for the Palace drains and so it made perfect sense to make it plain and ordinary. Steep crooked steps led from the back door, down from the escarpment, to the Kairatos Valley. It was this level space down by the river that Evans thought was the bullring.

In its time the Palace of Minos must have been perceived as a supernatural edifice. For Evans it was "a crescendo of spacious corridors, peristyles and halls, served beyond by a stately staircase." For others, it was not the opulent seat of a fair-minded and famous sovereign, but rather a house of death, built for the veneration and burial of the dead. Those few are convinced that it was merely an ancient cemetary, a remnant of a cult for the dead.

For Ritsos, it was poetic inspiration and the source of a lusty new dance first performed by Theseus and the youth of Athens:

> "... a new extraordinary dance with criss-crossing steps
> that repeated perhaps,
> in the strong noon light, the dark turns of the Labyrinth
> and, perhaps
> who knows what - the birds and the cicadas made so

much noise in the small nearby pine forest -
you couldn't make it out, you were dizzy from the sun
and the reflections from the sea,
a fine powdered glass, and the dazzling movements of
the naked bodies -
an extraordinary dance ...."[2]

No one knows precisely how the Minoans lived but from the finds it appears that Evan's vision rings true. And no one knows how they died or why their end was marked with sudden finality, such that no trace was left on their immediate descendants.

One theory of their demise is that more powerful foreigners, the Achaeans or the Dorians, conquered the island, subjugating the Minoans until they lost their identity. Another theory is that they caused their own destruction by internal strife, but no signs of this were ever found.

What is known is that by about 1400 B.C. all of Crete was decimated by some catastrophe. Some believe Crete was weakened by an earlier Mycenaean attack which destroyed their defenses, killed their spirit and left them hopelessly vulnerable to a second fatal attack. A more radical theory postpones the end to 1200 B.C. and attributes the downfall to the later Dorian invaders who also devastated the mainland.

The popular theory today originated with the late Greek archaeologist Spyridon Marinatos who theorized that the Minoan downfall took place before 1450 B.C. and resulted from the volcanic eruptions on the nearby island of Thera. It is this theory that tour guides announce in their presentations at Knossos.

The smell of decay, the heavy air of melancholy now permeate the abandoned Palace. The princes and the princesses and La Belle Parisienne are sadly gone, but their "venerable melancholy" is oddly felt:

---

[2]. Translated by Nikos Stangos, *Yannis Ritsos Selected Poems* (Athens: Efstathiadis Group, 1983), p. 125.

"... They are digging in the fields, the weeds have grown wild, and she, in a corner of the garden, in venerable melancholy ..."[3]

---

[3]. Translated by Kimon Friar, *Modern Greek Poetry* (Athens: Efstathiadis Group, 1982), Zisis Economou, "In the Palace of Knossos", p. 251.

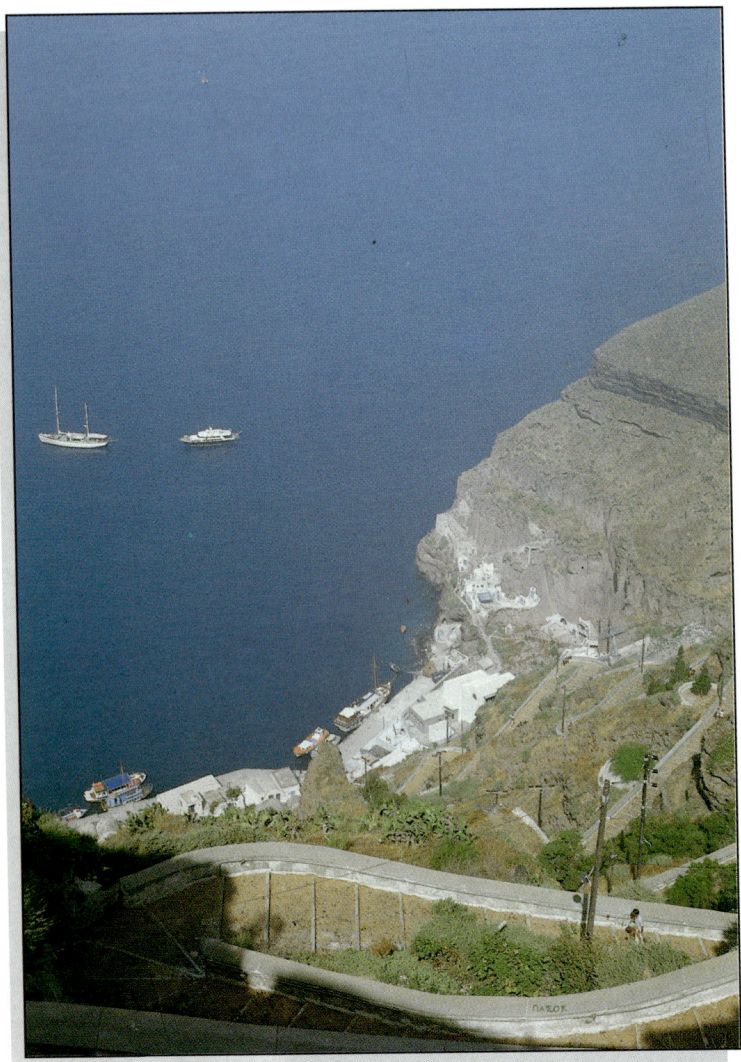

The bay below Phira.

2
THERA

The facade of the imposing structure, built of ashlar masonry, was plainly intended to inspire reverence. The large ornamented rooms suggest a great hall where homage was once paid to simple and sacred forms of life. Farther into town a more modest two-story house was made earthquake resistent with resilient olive-wood beams framing windows and doors. The domestic quarters occupied the second floor. The ground floor was reserved for a mill where grain was ground into flour then distributed to the townspeople.

In a neighboring structure adjacent to a large square, an elaborate frieze on the interior walls above the windows depicted a detailed scene of celebration. A fleet of ships is seen either returning from victory or returning home after a long absence at sea. The ships, paddled in the harbor by proud sailors, are surrounded by a colorful melange of exuberant life: undulating fish, a determined lion chasing a pair of frightened deer, large crocuses gracing the festoons of the ships and military men in .helmets, holding upright spears and keeping guard over their captains.

On the interior walls of other town structures frescoes depict elaborately dressed women with wavy dark hair flowing down their backs, lips and cheeks glowing with vibrant color, hoop earrings dangling immodestly from their ears, and other fine jewelry adorning their unquestioned beauty. And in another place, a fresco commemorates the awakening of spring - lilies stubbornly sprouting and blooming from harsh, rock-strewn soil, blooms kissed by the hint of a warm seductive breeze, swallows flirtatiously mating - all in vivid hues of persimmon, ocher, earth green and sky blue.

This remarkable and wealthy town is hardly of recent vintage. The ashes of one of the world's most cataclysmic geophysical events - an event so violent and wrenching that it ravaged an entire civilization - created a time vault that preserved life for milleniums in rich and graphic detail. It is the studied and skillful archaeological hand that is now brushing away the milleniums to uncover the astonishing beauty of Bronze Age Aktoriti, 1500 B.C.

It is theorized that millions of years ago the Greek peninsula, together with the Ionian Islands, the Aegean Islands and Asia Minor formed one contiguous land mass. The Greek Islands of today are the result of reverberations of explosive geological events. The sea was periodically racked by hugh catastrophic seismic and tidal waves that shifted and severed massive bodies of land. The island of Thera, one of the southernmost islands of the Cyclades in the Aegean, was formed by the issue of such violent seizures, by the aggregate lava and ash of many volcanic eruptions that spewed upon the sea then settled impermanently into a single round mass. Its initial shape determined its early name, Stronghyle, meaning "the round one."

Over the centuries following its formation, the local volcanos of Stronghyle remained relatively quiescent. Moreover, the volcanic soil was very fertile and it favored vegetation. There idyllic natural conditions fostered an advanced and refined civilization.

Peace, however, came to an abrupt and dramatic end. After a long period of relative quiet, the island was seized by an earthquake. or perhaps a series of earthquakes of uncertain magnitude, followed about a year later by an unprecedented volcanic eruption. The eruption triggered the uncompromising collapse and disappearance of the whole center of the island. The unfathomable dislocation of this massive land mass caused *tunamis* or sea waves which had disasterous effects on adjacent coasts and are believed to have been felt as far away as Crete.

The island, once the abundant shape of a full moon, is now a mere crescent, and at its southernmost tip is the town of Aktotiri. This crescent, along with a collection of uninhabited islets of pumice and ash that appear and disappear in its bay, were known commonly and collectively as Thera until the Middle Ages, when the Venetians named it Santorini.

Seferis poignantly captured the tragic and temporal beauty of

View of the shirred cliffs of Thera with the town of Phira as the crown

Sun-drenched Phira

Santorini in a poem by the same name:

> "... We found ourselves naked on the pumice stone
> watching the rising islands
> watching the red islands sink
> into their sleep, into our sleep.
> Here we found ourselves naked, holding the scales that
> tipped towards injustice.
> ..."[4]

The Early Excavations

Excavations which evidenced Minoan life on Santorini date back to the nineteenth century. Ironically, it may have been the disruptive work of a vast commercial construction project which inadvertently drew the attention of the scientific world to the pumice of Thera.

In the 1860s, new harbor installations were needed at Port Said because of the construction of the Suez Canal. The ideal material for these installations was a substance that was both durable and highly resistent to seawater. It was determined that three parts of pumice dust (pozzolana) mixed with one part of lime produced the required substance. It was further discovered that Thera contained a seemingly inexhaustible supply of pumice dust. The Suez Canal Company extracted vast quantities of this blackened dust from the interior of the crescent north of Akrotiri, from Cape Tinos on northeast Therasia (one of the volcanic islets in the bay), and from the cliffs all over the south face of Therasia. In some of these areas stone blocks frustrated the quarrying operations. These blocks, as even an untrained eye could see, were in fact the upper surfaces of ancient walls. It was undisputed that precious archaeological material was hauled off and destroyed during these inexorable quarrying operations.

---

4. Translated by Edmurd Keeley and Philip Sherrard, *George Seferis Collected Poems* (Princeton: Princeton University Press, 1981).

Some scientific work was initiated by dogged Greek residents. Alafousos, owner of a site on Therasia, and Nomicos, a local doctor, succeeded in getting an excavation started. They uncovered a house with several rooms and several pieces of decorated pottery.

In January 1866 a volcanic eruption roused Thera and attracted the attention of geologists and other scientists. Professor Christomanos, a professor of chemistry at Athens University ventured to Thera to study the eruption. He drew attention to the walls on Therasia and deduced that they were anterior to the formation of the pumice layer; at that time most believed that the walls were posterior tombs.

A French geologist, M. Fouqué, was also there to study the eruption and became intrigued with the ancient walls and pottery that had been found in the mines at Therasia. Although not a trained archaeologist, he recognized the significance of what had been unearthed and he called in others to help him excavate. He found what

View of the bay which swallowed the whole of the center of the island of Thera

may have been a Minoan farmhouse and the remains of an old man who apparently never made it to safety when disaster struck his island. Fouqué discontinued work on Therasia when it became too dangerous to continue excavating under tons of crumbling ash. His interest turned to Aktotiri.

The ash on Akrotiri was so eroded that Fouqué easily spotted ancient walls projecting from the sloping hillsides. A peasant led him to a nearby ravine. From his description of that ravine in *Santorin et ses Eruptions,* published in Paris in 1879, it is evident that it is the site of present excavations.

Fouqué records finding segments of walls in Aktoriti which matched walls found in Therasia. Although he yearned to excavate in Akrotiri in 1867, an unfortunate misunderstanding with the Greek property owner prevented him from ever doing so. He did, however, continue his field survey in the same area and found a layer of vase fragments. Further digging revealed shards which he later assembled into incomplete but discernible vases. In another ravine he was shown two small vaulted tombs which had been plundered.

Fouqué noted that he found carbonized vegetables such as barley, peas and lentils in clay pots and olive-wood beams in houses that were remarkably well preserved. He concluded that the ash layer had been remarkably impervious to water penetration.

The discoveries of Fouqué led to a more formal excavation conducted by Mamet and Gorceix who, with French support and Greek consent, excavated at Akrotiri in April and May 1870. Mamet's published findings, *De Insula Thera* (1874), do not identify place or property names, but from the precisely drawn maps it appears that the richest finds were from the east side of the ravine where the current excavations are taking place.

Among the finds were obsidian knives, scrappers, large storage jugs, a pure copper saw and structures with elegant frescoes, some of which faded upon exposure to light. From these and other finds the French archaeologists concluded that the residents of Akrotiri produced lime to make plaster, used weights and measures, pos-

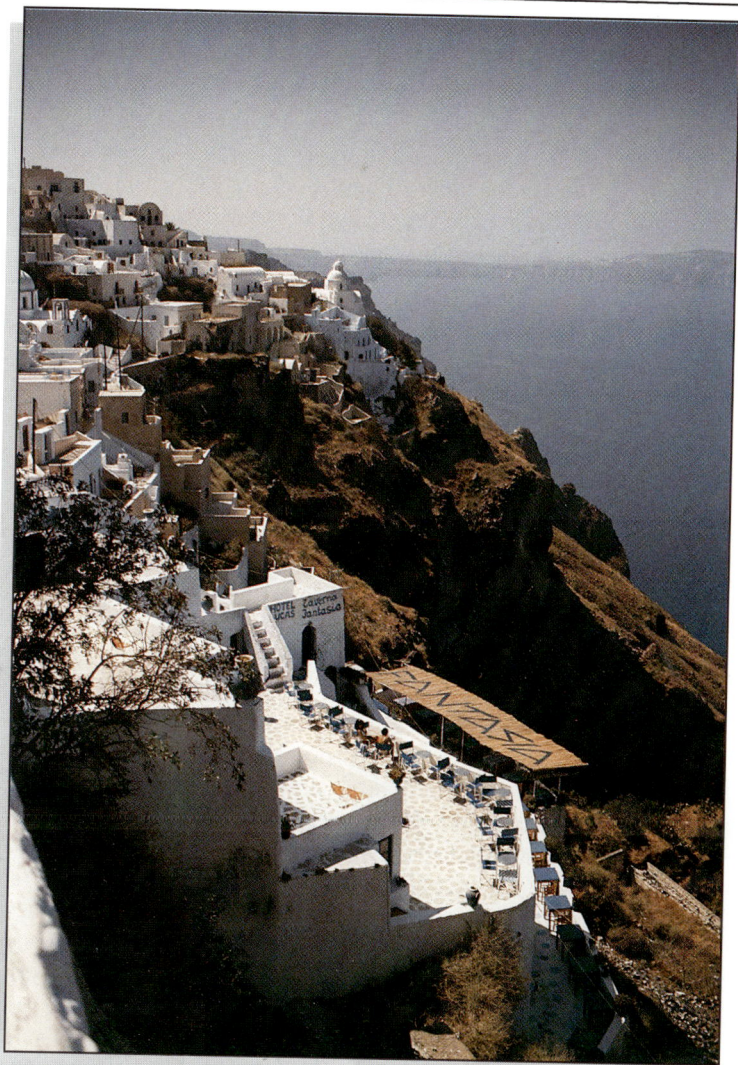

View of the bay below Phira with the volcanic islets in the distance, a constant reminder of Thera's geophysical past

sessed a system of numeration, built vaults and made impressive polychromatic frescoes. They learned too that agriculture flourished and that weaving and pottery-making were highly advanced skills.

After the 1870 excavations no further work was carried out on Thera until 1900. In that year Robert Zahn dug in the valley of Potomos, some distance from the current site of excavations in Akrotiri. Zahn never published his findings but he kept a diary and he published a photograph of a Minoan house that he excavated.

These early finds demonstrated that this ephemeral Aegean island had an advanced culture before it was annihilated by the devastating volcanic eruption and subsequent disaster. Following the destruction Akrotiri was spared for posterity. Thick blankets of pumice preserved that place in that time. The inhabitants have vanished without a trace, but their town remains as their grand memorial.

The Current Excavations

The current excavations at Akrotiri began in 1967 and have proceeded steadily since then. On May 25, 1967 Professor Spyridon Marinatos, for the Archaeological Society of Athens, in collaboration with Emily Vermeule of the Boston Museum of Fine Arts and James W. Mavor, Jr. of the Woods Hole Oceanographic Institute opened the first trial trench (Bronos I) in a field belonging to Calliope Bronos at a spot called Favata.

From the writings of Marinatos, Mavor and others, much is known of that first season. A villager directed them to the place where they first excavated. Following the spring rains the villager had found fragments of large pots and storage jars in a ravine south of the field where he planted tomatoes. His observations proved fruitful. On the very first day of the excavations, in the place where the fragments had been seen, the upper surfaces of ancient walls appeared and a lamp was found with soot still visible on its rim. Marinatos theorized that the inhabitants of Akrotiri probably burned animal fat with the lamp. In most places at that time, with the exception of Crete, olive oil was too precious to burn. It was suggested that the lamp was used to anoit the body for protection from the sun and for libation to the gods.

A donkey cave became the site of the second trenche (Alvaniti I). Mavor reported that a local villager, George Aliveros, recounted that he had seen the floor of the donkey cave collapse, revealing what appeared to be a chamber or room below. He had similarly seen a section of an adjacent field sink in as if resting on a hollow cavity. A trench about thirty feet long and ten feet deep yielded little at first, but as the excavators reached the ash-pumice layer, approximately fifteen feet deep, a slab of hand-cut limestone was found. Nearby a cylindrical stone base for a wooden column was found; it was determined to be similar to the type found in the reconstruction of the Palace of Minos in Knossos, Crete.

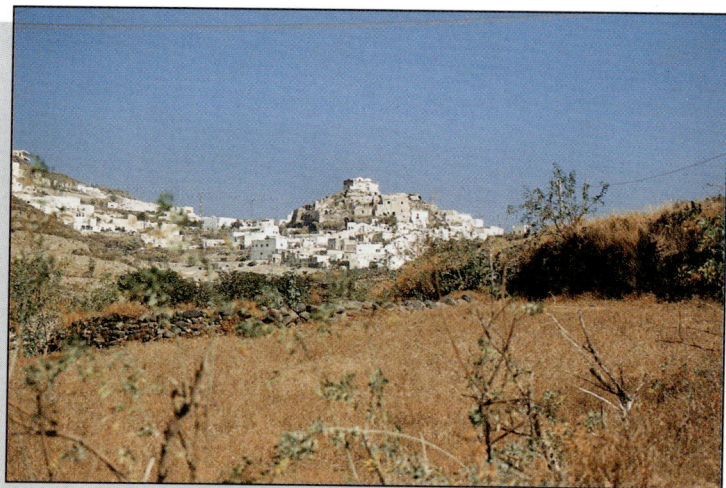

The town of Akrotiri on Thera

The next day in Alvaniti I a large quantity of shards were found. Walls and then a large window appeared. A second-story window was uncovered. Two additional exploratory trenches indicated two additional two-story structures. It was evident that they had found the right place.

After a brief interruption digging resumed June 21, 1967 in Arvaniti I. They found a low window that led to a room where notable finds were made. Along the south side of the room were six or seven enormous storage jars or *pithoi,* still standing and unbroken, some painted in red, brown or black and some decorated in a rope design. Marinatos called the room a storeroom. Along the west side of the room jugs, a stone mortar, stone lamps and a large cooking pot resting on three legs were found alongside a low square hearth. The jars may have served as storage bins for oil, corn and other vegetables.

Jars, jugs and pottery were undoubtedly preserved by the dense layers of pumice. One painted jar that had toppled over during the ancient disaster was discovered in that same position near the low window. It was believed that it had fallen through the shattered second floor to the ground floor which had been blanketed with cushioning pumice. Although cracked, it was not broken. It was found to contain loom weights and volcanic stones.

The finds of the 1967 season were harbingers of what was yet uncovered. These finds were unquestionably remarkable. During that first season approximately nine trenches were dug and countless donkey-loads of artifacts were transported from the excavation site to the museum in Phira, the capital of the island. Below the sloping ash-covered ravine where generations of villagers planted tomatoes and grew grapes, where Greek children played and donkeys brayed, a great town waited to be discovered.

Professor Marinatos presided over these excavations from 1967 to his untimely death. Professor Doumas now continues that work. As the pumice layers are carefully removed each year, evidence of life in ancient Akrotiri is still emerging. Who were these people? Where did they go? Why did they not return?

The archaeological site at Akrotiri on Thera

The archaeological site at Akrotiri protectively covering the ancient ruins

Although it was initially supposed that the townspeople fled in haste from impending disaster, it is now believed that they were somehow forced to leave their homes well before the volcano erupted. Seeds which were left on the ruins of the houses had begun to germinate when the first hot ashes rained down. The residents had adequate warning, time to flee, time to gather their valuables and time to exodus en masse by sea. They took their jewelry, their bronzes, their seal-stones and they fled. No human skeletal remains have yet been found. And with the exception of a pig skeleton, no animal skeletons were found.

It should be noted that there is evidence that some residents lingered behind after most had gone. It was discovered that objects had been moved on the pumice layer indicating that people were present at the time of the eruption. They too fled without a trace. Apparently they escaped unscathed as well. Marinatos named them troglodytes (dwellers in the ruins).

What kind of town was Akrotiri? The archaeological material presents a wealthy town. Despite the organized removal of all valuables by the fleeing residents, the magnificence of the structures, the quality of the pottery and the sheer beauty of the frescoes substantiate the presence of importance and wealth. The precious frescoes have been removed from the site and are now on exhibit in a special air-cooled room in the National Archaeological Museum in Athens.

The architecture reveals a hierarchic system. Some structures are imposing, others modest. Some appear to serve communal needs, others are isolated, removed and reverent. The domestic quarters are quite separate from work areas, although they typically shared the same structure. The domestic quarters are richly decorated on the upper stories. The ground floors were reserved for places of labor, such as pottery workshops, lapidaries, metal workshops and mills to grind grain into flour. In areas where mills were located, a large low window often overlooked a large square where the floor was conveniently distributed to the townspeople. Although wooden objects themselves do not survive, imprints of ornate furniture were found in ash. Some furniture, beds, stools, and a table, have been reconstructed from molds made from the ash imprints.

Kitchens have been identified by the discovery of hearths and cooking pots. Some kitchens appear to belong to a community of families because the cooking pots are too numerous to belong to a single family unit. Communal meals were also inferred. In addition, large storage areas were uncovered. These may have been used to serve the needs of the community and may evidence a type of collective economy.

The ancient diet can be gleaned from the remains of the food and from the depictions of life in the frescoes. Grain, lentils, beans, pulses, pigs, goats, deer and sheep were found to have been included in their diets.

Akrotiri cannot be studied in isolation. Its relationship to other civilizations has inevitably become the subject of much discourse. The most discussed topics are its relationship with Minoan Crete and with the legend of the lost Atlantis.

Professor Marinatos considered the relationship between Thera and Crete as early as the 1930s. While excavating a Minoan villa in Amnissos, Crete, he believed that an earthquake was the cause for the devastation he found. He quickly abandoned that theory, however, when he discovered pumice. He then concluded that what had destroyed Minoan Crete was not an earthquake at all, but rather a massive eruption of the volcano at Thera. His theory was published in a work entitled, "The Volcanic Destruction of Minoan Crete." Although his theory did not convince all of his colleagues at that time, Marinatos persisted and believed that if he excavated in Thera and found pottery there of the same period as that of the Minoan villas and palaces of Crete, his theory would be validated. Following the archaeological finds in Akrotiri, Marinatos concluded that the coastal settlements of Crete were destroyed by the *tunamis* which flowed from the massive dislocation of the center of Thera at a time which he placed at about 1520 B.C. Although his theory still lacks unanimous support, it is conceded that the pottery in Akrotiri is almost contemporaneous with that of Minoan Crete.

Regardless of whether or not it is conclusively proved that Thera is indeed Atlantis or that the civilizations of Thera and Crete were allied, the significance of these finds is unimpeachable.

Walking through this ancient town, much as the ancient residents did, inevitably inspires visions of fleeting time. Over three thousand years have passed and yet we are more alike than different. We laugh we love we eat. We are equally vulnerable to nature's fury, equally touched by the budding beauty of a spring day and equally transitory.

And thoughts of our desire for immortality surface. Soon our time will pass. Will our legacy be as grand? Will it be a pebble, inscribed with our name, resting on the bottom of the sea. Or will we slip into a dreamless sleep and vanish without a trace. Seferis understood too well:

> "... Bend if you can to the dark sea forgetting the sound
> of a flute on naked feet that trod your sleep in the other,
> the sunken life.
> Write if you can on your last shell the day the name the
> place and fling it into the sea so that it sinks."

3
GORTYN

The Greek islands float like buoyant mounds of ancient rock, anchored tenaciously in the Aegean Sea. Insular rocky ridges of land crumble into bits of stone that "soak in the light and memory."[5] Stones become markers for a villager's property line, for "something in his field, in the cemetary, in the wall, in the woods."[6]

In 1857 Thenon found one such stone from an ancient buried wall in southcentral Crete, in the town of Gortyn, centered in the Plain of Messara, between Ayii Deka and Metropolis. The inscription on that stone perplexed scholars for decades following Thenon's acquisition of it for the Louvre. Twenty-seven years later the decipherment of the etchings on that stone led to the discovery of the earliest Greek and the first European law code. It is identified as belonging to the fifth century B.C. The hugh inscribed blocks of stone are known collectively as the Code of Gortyn.

"And if a husband and wife should be divorced, she is to have her own property which she came with to her husband and half of the produce, if there be any from her own property, and half of whatever she has woven within, whatever there may be, plus five staters if the husband be the cause of the divorce; but if the husband should declare that he is not the cause, the judge is to decide on oath. And if she should carry away anything else belonging to the husband, she shall pay five staters and whatever she may carry away; and let her restore whatever she may have filched; but as regards things which she denies (the judge) shall decree that the woman take an oath of denial by Artemis, before the statue of the Archeress in the Amyklaian temple. And whatever anyone else may take from her after she has made her oath of denial, he shall pay the thing itself plus five staters. If a stranger should help her in packing off, he shall pay ten

---

[5]. "Stones", Translated by Nikos Stagnos, *Yannis Ritsos: Selected Poems* (Athens, Efstathiadis Group, 1983), p. 43.

[6]. *Id.*

staters and double the value of whatever the judge swears he helped to pack off."[7]

This portion of the ancient legislation relating to the division of property upon divorce, curiously resembles modern California law, which preserves each spouse's separate property and which provides for a division of the fruits of each spouse's labors for the duration of the marriage. Unlike modern law, however, the sharing of ancient community property was not reciprocal. The Cretan husband obtained one-half the produce of his wife's labors from the marital period at the time of divorce, but he was not obligated to share the fruits of his own labors with his divorced wife.

This ancient law expressly protected the couple's separate property. Any dowry that the wife had received from her family at the time of her marriage, or any inheritance that she had received during the marriage remained under her control. Her husband could neither sell nor mortgage it. These ancient family laws, however, unquestionably favored the husband. Anything that the husband added to his separate property by his own efforts remained his own, but, under certain conditions, that which the wife added to hers could be taken from her by her ancient spouse.

The Gortyn Code has been loftily described by some writers as the Queen of Inscriptions or the Twelve Tablets of Gortyn. It is rightly acknowledged to be the original source of modern laws. The laws are etched in elegant Doric Greek, the youngest of the pre-historic dialects of the Greek language which was introduced to the Greek speaking area by one of successive migrations. It is dated between 480-460 B.C. and although the date most often cited is 450 B.C., the precise date of the inscription remains unknown. Moreover, the exact date of the original legislation is yet undetermined.

Legal precepts are generally regarded as reflective of the more conservative tenets of a society and thus it is theorized that this ancient Code incorporated unwritten pre-historic conventions, sanctions and practices that long predate the actual etching of the inscription. These early practices were assimilated in the Code just

---

[7]. Translated by Ronald F. Willetts, *The Law Code of Gortyn.* pp. 40-41.

as the verse of Homer embodied prior memorized oral beliefs. In ancient Crete, as in Sparta, laws were memorized and transmitted orally from generation to generation. As such, the Code undoubtedly incorporated rules and regulations which evolved from very primitive times.

The entire inscription of laws once formed a massive concave wall that was an integral part of the structure of an ancient building. If the construction of the wall had continued to form a circle, it would have had a diameter of about a hundred feet. The laws were engraved in large blocks of grey limestone which cut through four layers of stone.

Evidence has been found that suggests that a fifth layer of stone existed when the inscription was first etched. In 1900 a stone was found on the site which had once formed part of the wall. It was broken into two parts and was inscribed with the end of column XI and sequentially numbered. Other parts of the inscription have also

The plane tree where the sons of Zeus and Europa were born - Minos, Rhadamanthys and Sarpedon

Back view of the Roman Odeum at Gortyn

South wall of the Roman Odeum showing alcoves at Gortyn

The Code of Gortyn

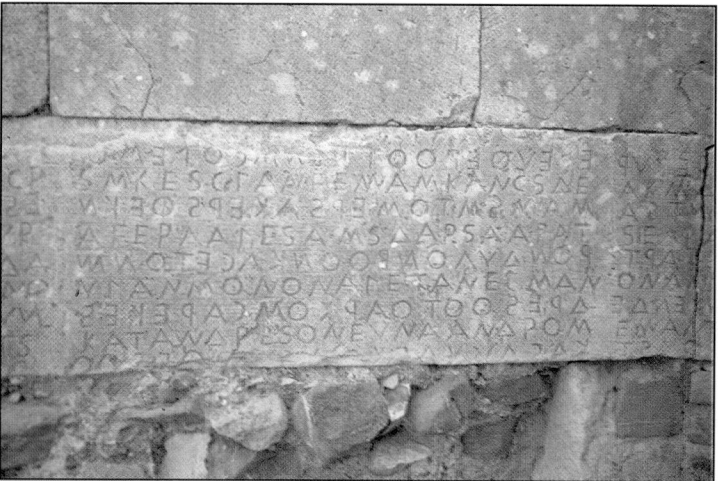

View of the lettering of the laws etched in stone in Gortyn

been found to have incomplete lines, presumably because the deepest portion of the etched lettering of these lines had been cut upon the fifth layer of stone from the original building.

The inscribed blocks rest upon a broad base and are stacked one atop the other to a height of about five feet. The four carefully hewn blocks on which the inscription is etched are crowned with a blank row. On the end is a projecting pilaster and the final column of laws has spaced unfilled, like the last page of the final chapter of a book.

From what appears to be an original numbering system in the margins it was inferred that the whole inscription has been found, except for a portion of the top left corner of column IX and nearly the entire top portions of columns X and XII. Parts of the top row of blocks were removed or broken when a mill stream was made.

The building which contained the laws underwent several architectural modifications. The curved wall of laws once supported the structure of a first century B.C. theatre. The inscription was salvaged and preserved by the Romans when they incorporated the Code in their buildings. The laws then became an integral and respected part of a Roman period Odeion or covered theatre.

It is probable that the wall once formed part of a more ancient building, perhaps an early court of law. As some related fragments of the inscription have been found in the surrounding area, it is believed that the original building on the site was indeed a court of law and the large precision-cut laws once lined the formidable courtroom walls. Fortunately, the wall was appreciated and preserved through the generations and was protectively incorporated in each successive building.

The legislation is engraved with approximately seventeen thousand letters arranged in twelve columns. The length of the whole concave inscription measures about thirty feet from end to end. Each column, except the last, consists of more than fifty lines, the whole amounting to more than six hundred lines.

The letters of the Code, with few exceptions, are very distinctly imprinted. In some parts of the wall, however, the seams of the blocks interrupt the clarity of the letters and the letters appear obscured or damaged. The lettering is about an inch high and is written in an alphabet of only eighteen letters and in a dialect little known from other writings or inscriptions. Scholars have noted that the development of the alphabet in Crete lagged behind other areas, thereby making the ancient Cretan dialect more difficult to decipher.

The words of the laws flow successively without interruption, without spaces between the words and without breathing or accent marks. Many word forms were apparently newly created grammatical clusters and some words may have been created when the laws were first produced. In a few places the words are utterly illegible and indecipherable.

Gaps can be discerned in the inscription where the etcher chose to leave blanks in surface faults or imperfections in the stone. Corrections are also evident in the cutting of the letters. While most scholars agree that the bulk of the inscription was cut by the same skilled engraver, it is also widely held that the final section of the Code was cut by a different hand.

The Code provides an illuminating view of the actual legislation in force in ancient Crete. By contrast, other early legislation, such as the Roman Code, is unknown in any authentic manner. A few barely intelligible fragments, collectively expressed by writers centuries after the laws were in force, and a few general statements of common law constitute our cumulative knowledge of that Code. By contrast, the Gortyn Code cuts through centuries of scholarly speculation and imprecise sources to an actual look at one of the earliest examples of comprehensive lawmaking. By its extent and character, the Code remains an authentic prototype of all legal inscriptions, either of ancient Italy or of ancient Greece.

Scholars have been able to date the Code based upon the style of the alphabet, the use of distinctive Doric Greek, the unique configuration of the letters, the available linguistic data and the relevant evidence from original numismatic sources. In addition, the manner in which the writing was carved, starting at the top from right to left, left to right, alternatively, known as the ox-plough or *boustrophedon* pattern, allowed scholars to more precisely date the Code.

The laws that have been found are not a complete Code. They probably supplement or amend a body of common law that had been promulgated orally and memorialized in prior written law. The laws codify regulations relating to highly pragmatic matters such as the disposition of property or children upon divorce or death as well as ensure the integrity of individual civil liberties for the various social classes. The legislation that has been found embraces a broad range of topics. The Code is admirable for its simplicity of expression and for its practical wisdom.

The formulation of laws evolves from one precedent which follows another, then another; soon these precedents accumulate and constitute law. Similarly, the inevitable predicaments of life in early Crete were resolved piecemeal at first, one precedent after another. A pattern of justice then emerged that was preserved in written form, then etched forever in blocks of stone. In its magnitude, its precision, its systematic collection of statutes, the Code is unequaled.

The discovery of the Code was a gradual process that spanned some twenty-seven years. In 1857 Thenon found an inscribed stone built into the walls of a mill beside the banks of the Lethaios, a river that flowed through Gortyn. After Thenon purchased the stone for the Louvre, it captured the attention of interested scholars. Many were intrigued by the obscure inscription. It appeared so ancient, so unfathomable. In 1878, however, Bréal deciphered the meaning of that first fragment of the Code and determined that it related to the adoption of children.

In 1879 in Crete, Haussoulier copied a similar fragment which he discovered in a house near the same mill. He determined that its meaning related to the rights of heiresses.

Then in July 1884, Dr. Frederico Halbherr, an Italian scholar known for his later excavations at Phaistos, visited the site in Gortyn at a fortuitous time when the water level was low alongside the mill. When he first realized that a significant building (the Odeion) was just beneath the water's surface, he was cooling off from the hot Cretan sun, washing his feet in the Lethaios which ran just over the upper portion of the engraved wall.

Some imprinted letters were shown to Halbherr who then made a trench along the inside of the wall. He then discovered four inscribed columns. The last column on the left was not completely inscribed at the bottom. This indicated that it was the end of the whole inscription in that direction. In the opposite direction, however, the inscription continued through a field where Halbherr sought permission to dig from the Cretan landowner. His request was denied.

The fragment of the inscription that had thus far been uncovered had been cut directly upon the layers of stone in the wall with great precision. The two fragments that had been copied by Thenon and Haussoulier had come from the same stream. The scholars quickly concluded that these first two fragments had been taken from the

View of the orchestra of the Roman Odeum at Gortyn

same wall and had in fact formed the upper layers of an ancient writing.

Within two days of their discovery, Halbherr had copied the four columns he had found. He then went to Iraklion where he met Dr. Ernst Fabricius who had been traveling in western Crete on behalf of the German Institute of Athens. He told Fabricius about his discovery and requested that Fabricius go to Gortyn to see it for himself. Fabricius arrived in Gortyn at the end of October and persuaded the recalcitrant Cretan property owner to allow him to dig a trench along the wall to the limit of the inscription. He found eight more columns that were beautifully preserved. With more of the wall exposed, it could be seen that the wall on which the twelve columns of the Code had been etched was curved, and that, if the circle had been closed, it would have been an imposing structure.

Halbherr and Fabricius then compared their copies with the original before the wall was obscured again by the stream. They communicated their copies with each other and published their findings separately.

Fabricius and Comparetti were responsible for the first publication of what has come to be known as the First Gortyn Code, and other editions, translations and commentaries have followed. The Second Code, only part of a few columns of which survive, of about the same date, completes the sum of what is now referred to under the general heading of the Gortyn Code.

The Code addressed a broad range of civil issues, including marriage and divorce, adoption, rape, adultery, inheritance, the rights of heiresses and the rights of the mother and of the daughter. The area of family law predominates. Although the offense of rape is included, it is treated as a private civil wrong and not a criminal offense.

There were clearly defined classes of people, such as the free citizens, those entitled to all rights, and the *apetairoi,* a sub-category of free citizens who were not entitled to full status and who were excluded from political rights. The remaining two classes were the serfs and the slaves. The fines imposed for various offenses and the quantum of evidence required for proof varied depending upon the accused's social class. Generally, the most severe fines were imposed upon those who committed crimes against free citizens.

The word *dromeus* as used in the Code was a "runner", or an adult who had acquired the right to exercise in the public gymnasium. *Apodromos* was a young boy still excluded from the public athletic exercises. Although it is not clearly defined in the Code, it is believed that a young man became a *dromeus* at the age of twenty. When he did gain that status, he became a citizen and was vested with certain legal responsibilities and there was a presumption that he became a competent witness.

The laws were organized by subject matter. Subjects which were addressed by the legislation included the rights of the accused, both free citizens and slaves, and the penalties for rape, seduction and adultery for the different social classes. Additional subjects included the disposition of the separate and community property of a

The stage of the Roman Odeum at Gortyn

married couple during marriage and upon divorce, the disposition of property and children upon the death of either spouse, the disposition of children born after divorce or out of wedlock, the division of property among children upon death of the father or mother, the sale and mortgage of family property, the marriage of an heiress to a husband appointed by law and the disposition of her property. Other related topics were also included.

The first law etched in the first column, and perhaps regarded by the ancient Gortynians as first in importance, related to the rights of the accused before trial. It may be a forerunner of the presumption of innocence, the bedrock of Anglo-American law:

> "Whoever may be likely to contend about a free man or a slave is not to seize him before trial. But if he make seizure, let (the judge) condemn him to (a fine of) ten staters for a free man, five for a slave of whomsoever he does seize and let him give judgment that he release him within three days; but if he do not release him, let (the judge) condemn him to (a time of) a stater for a free man and a drachma for a slave, for each day until he do release him; and the judge is to decide on oath as to the time; but if he should deny the seizure, unless a witness should testify, the judge is to decide on oath."[8]

There was a presumption in Gortyn law in favor of free status for the accused. If testimony was presented in support of the accused's free status and conflicting testimony was also offered to prove that he was a slave, the evidence regarding free status was accorded greater weight. If the ownership of a slave was disputed by two alleged masters, the judge ruled in favor of the live testimony. If, however, two or more witnesses testified and conflicting testimony emerged, the judge decided "on oath". The judge was empowered with such discretionary authority in many instances in the Code and undoubtedly based the ruling on the credibility and demeanor of the various witnesses.

---

[8]. *Id.* at 39.

Rape and adultery were treated as companion civil offenses, each punishable by fines which were apportioned according to the social status of the victim, or, on occasion, by the class of the offender. The highest fines were imposed for rape of a free person by a slave or adultery between a slave and a free woman. Adultery which took place in the house of a free woman's father, brother or husband was the more grievous adulterous offense; if the act was consummated in some other place, the fine was diminished by one-half.

There is a provision for children born after divorce. The child was to be brought to the home of the ex-husband in the presence of three witnesses. If the father did not accept the child, the child's destiny then rested with the mother. She acquired the power to either rear it or "expose" it. Some have presumed that exposure is infanticide, but it may simply have meant that the child became available for adoption.

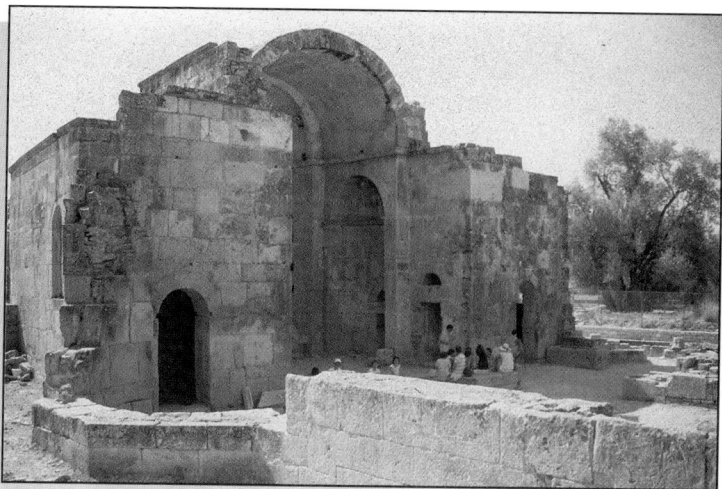

The basilica of St. Titus at Gortyn named for the first bishop of Crete

If the woman failed to present the child to the father and exposed the child nonetheless, she was charged with the offense and summoned to court. If she was convicted, her fine was doubled if the child was a free child.

The laws regulating the marriage of an heiress and the disposition of her property are considerably detailed. If the father died and had no male heirs, the daughters were the heiresses and they were required to marry in accordance with Gortyn law. The husband-to-be was preordained:

> "The heiress is to be married to the brother of her father, the oldest of those living. And, if there be more heiresses and brothers of the father, they are to be married to the next oldest. And if there should be no brothers of the father, but sons of the brothers, she is to be married to that one (who is the son) of the oldest. And if there should be more heiresses and sons of brothers, they are to be married to the next after the son of the oldest. The groomelect is to have one heiress and not more."[9]

If the heiress was too young to marry (The age of puberty was generally regarded as age twelve for a girl and fourteen for a boy), she was given her father's house and her betrothed received one-half the revenue from the estate. If the intended groom chose to delay the marriage, assuming they were both old enough to marry, on the grounds that he was still a minor, all the property remained in the heiress' control until the marriage. If upon maturity her betrothed continued to resist marriage and she, by contrast, remained eager and willing, "the relatives of the heiress are to bring the matter to court and the judge is to order the marriage to take place within two months." If he still balks at the marriage after the court order, the heiress must marry the next in succession. If no other groom-elect existed in the hierarchy prescribed by law, she was then free to

---

[9]. *Id.* at 45

marry whom she wished "of those who ask from the tribe." The marriage of the heiress was dictated by the law and by the willingness of her father's relatives to have her. Only if and when that designated group of paternal uncles and first cousins was exhausted was she free to choose among those unappointed suitors who had asked.

It has been noted with some interest that homicide provisions are absent from the Code. Prior written legislation may have addressed the offense or perhaps the early Cretan society simply resorted to self-help. Given the highly detailed consideration given to the other predictable dilemmas of life which do appear in the Code, it may well be that a companion criminal code was in existence at the time which imposed public punishment for homicide and other crimes.

· The Gortyn law mandated that the father had control of the children and of the division of property among them; the mother maintained control over her own property only. When the father died the bulk of the inheritance went to the sons. That included the houses in the town and the contents of country houses, provided that they were not occupied by a serf, and the sheep and larger animals not belonging to a serf.

The remaining property was divided. The sons received two parts, the daughters one part each. The mother's property was similarly divided.

If the people who make the law are harsh and strict, the law itself will be rigorous and probably unjust. The Gortyn Code shows a gentler touch, imbued with much wisdom and much humanity. For example, it imposed fines for assaults by free persons upon slaves. It also provided that the slave, *katekeimenos,* who carried away another's crops or used another's land, pursuant to the order of his master, was not liable. The master alone was liable. The Gortyn law also protected the slave against robbery by his master. The sheep and cattle which belonged to a serf were not regarded as part of the master's estate and the master could not take them from the serf.

Slaves were permitted to appeal to the courts for protective orders from their masters and to prosecute civil actions against them.

Female slaves were entitled to seek damages from their masters if they were victims of the master's assaults. The slave-woman was not only permitted to take oath to an assault upon her by her master, but also her oath in such cases prevailed over that of her master.

The serfs and their wives had legitimate legal and social status. A serf could marry and divorce. When a female serf married, she changed masters and became subject to her husband's master. If she divorced, she was returned to her former master.

The name Gortyn is believed to be the name of the ancient founder of the town. Prior names of the site include Helliotis, Larisa and Kremnis.

Many myths are associated with Gortyn. One such myth is that Zeus, transformed into a gallant white bull, carried on his back the beautiful princess Europa across the seas from her home in Phoenicia to the island of Crete. Their marriage was contracted beneath an evergreen plane tree beside the Lethaios in Gortyn. Modern Cretan tour guides point to an existing plane tree in Gortyn and extol its extraordinary nature. It is, they urge, the same mythic tree. While other trees in Crete shed their leaves in winter, this anomaly maintains a steady cycle of new growth and boasts in mid-winter a full dress of new leaves. Is that not sufficient evidence, they ask, of its supernatural past? From the marriage of Zeus and Europa that took place under the plane tree, three famous sons were born. They became the ruling kings of Crete: Minos of Knossos, Rhadamantys of Phaistos and Sarpedon of Malia.

Gortyn dominates the Messara Plain, the largest and most fertile plain in Crete and used by the Romans as one of their principal granaries. When Crete became a Roman province the provincial capital was first Knossos, then Gortyn, the city that had offered the least resistance to the conquerors. The Roman praetor or proconsul governed the province from Gortyn, which then became so populated that it was estimated to have a population of about 300,000.

A neighboring town to the east, Ayii Deka, is named for the "holy ten" who were beheaded for refusing to abandon their Christian faith for the Roman gods. A Byzantine church, dedicated to the ten martyrs, was built there in about 250, from material obtained from the ruins of Gortyn.

In the *Iliad,* Homer listed Gortyn as the second largest city in Crete, after Knossos. There are, however, no significant finds from Dorian Knossos.

The archaeological finds from Gortyn are broadly scattered for nearly a mile, from an acropolis on a foothill to a classical stadium just beyond the perimeter of the town wall. The excavations were mainly conducted by the Italians with the assistance of a few Greek archaeologists. The crown of the acropolis was a classical temple. Votive offerings were buried on the steep slope and span from the post-Palace period in Crete to the Roman times. At the foot of the acropolis was a classical theatre and across the Lethaios was the agora or marketplace. The town actually had two theatres, two fountains and Nymphaia, shrines to the nymphs, the agora with an Asklepion, and a stadium with large public baths. The Gortyn Code and the round building in which it was first etched became a part of the Roman Odeum, the finer of the two covered theatres.

The first building most modern visitors are shown is the basilica of St. Titus, the patron saint of the island and the first bishop of Crete. Titus was a leader of early Christians in Crete and St. Paul, who may have gone to Gortyn, wrote an epistle to Titus. The basilica is from the sixth century and was built over the tomb of St. Titus. The configuration of the church, divided into three aisles, is representative of early Christian architecture. The apse is still in good condition and traces of early frescoes are visible in a side chapel.

Beyond the church is the Roman agora with the roofed Roman Odeum. The Odeum was reconstructed by the emperor Trajan around 100 A.D. and in it, on the face of the interior north wall, were the etched blocks of laws. The Odeum was a very important building to the Romans. The orchestra was paved with patterned designs of black and white marble. In the south wall were alcoves for a collection of statues.

Across the stream and opposite the Odeum are the remains of a second theatre built on the slope of the hill. On the top of the acropolis was the temple to Apollo. On the other side of the road the remains of a Roman town cover a vast area. Most of the area remains unexcavated.

The temple of Pythian Apollo is the main temple and served at one time as the state treasury. The temple was modified many times. In the seventh century B.C. only the square cella existed. The external walls were then covered with inscriptions. In 200 B.C. a pronaos with six Doric columns were added. This was later divided into three aisles by two colonnades of four Corinthian columns each. An altar and an apse can still be seen in the west wall.

A small temple to the north was dedicated to Isis and Serapis and other Egyptian deities who had begun to attract worshippers from throughout Europe.

An additional architectural remain is a large complex, The Praetorium, which once belonged to the Roman governor. The building contains a basilica with a row of columns, a portico with three apses and a peristyle court which was connected to the public baths.

The law is, as Holmes once said, a mirror, "a magic mirror wherein we see reflected not only our own lives but the lives of all men that have been." The Gortyn Code reflects the lives of those who lived in early Crete with awesome precision. No other tangible remnant of a man is more accurately reflective of who he was than his own words. From these fifth century B.C. words we know how fiercely protective these lawmakers were of their families, how fair to their slaves and how generous to their victims.

The blocks of etched limestone still stand where they were found but they are now protectively covered. And the laws themselves, foreseen by precient lawmakers centuries ago, still endure in part today.

> "And, through the heat of conflict, keeps the law
> In calmness made, and sees what he foresaw."[10]

---

[10]. William Wordsworth, "Character of the Happy Warrior," 1806.

4.
DELOS

His appetite for lovers is unrivaled. His finely chiseled face and long satisfying torso, models of manly beauty, are immortalized in marble. His ineffable sensuality inspired Byron and Shelley and aroused natural resentment in mortal men. His passions, however, were not entirely unchecked. His restiveness and vengeance caused Zeus to banish him for a time from heaven.

He returned the sunshine to spring, stroked the splayed meadows with golden nectar and made arid fields burst into bloom. He ended plagues, founded colonies and foresaw the future with astonishing exactitude. His oracles are renown. His first love is legend. Due to Cupid's spite it was an unrequited, unconsummated love, but one that never left him.

He chased her with such longing. She drew away with inexplicable indifference. One day his passion and determination overtook her. He seized her in his arms. When his breath was in her hair she grew stiff. Tender bark encircled her virgin breast. Her long dishevelled hair turned to silvery leaves, her arms young branches and her foot penetrated the earth and took root. The beautiful face became a delicate treetop. The young desired nymph metamorphosed in his arms to a laurel.

When she felt the grip of his inescapable embrace, when his warm breath penetrated her hair, she cried to her father to change her form, to withdraw from his reach forever.

Daphne drew beyond Apollo's grasp but remained with him always. Her tender leaves crowned his curling hair and tangled with the golden ringlets like gentle loving fingers. Her pliable branches adorned his harp and his quiver, and her garland was a prized wreath of attainment and triumph.

In "Child Harolde" Byron described the matchless god aglow in his victory over the serpent Python:

Approaching Delos by boat with Mount Cynthus in background

> "... The lord of the unerring bow,
> The god of Life, and poetry, and light,
> The Sun, in human limbs arrayed, and brow
> All radiant from his triump in the fight.
> The shaft has just been shot; the arrow bright
> With an immortal's vengeance; in his eye
> And nostril, beautiful disdain, and might
> And majesty flash their full lighting by,
> Developing in that one glance the Deity."

Delos prospered because of Apollo. The island's destiny was ordained when his mother, a wandering pregnant woman carrying the unborn son of Zeus, sought a kindly place to rest and give birth. Leto combed the earth in search of a maternal nest. Rivers and towns recoiled at her approach. They dared not risk the wrath of Hera, the spurned wife. Delos alone took her in. The small barren island accepted her with the promise that the child to be born would always cherish the place where he first saw light.

Poseidon is responsible for the legendary genesis of Delos. The powerful sea god created the island with his trident and raised it from the sea like some free-floating sponge. Unanchored, suspended on the sea, it was perpetually tossed by the waves and blown by fierce sea winds. It was Zeus who generously fastened the island to the bottom of the sea as a resting place for his beloved Leto. Beneath the island Zeus attached impenetrable pillars which anchored it to the depths of the Aegean. The Greeks believed with unswerving conviction that nothing in heaven or earth could ever move this sacred place because of the giant pillars of adamant which held it secure with divine trust.

Apollo was born as Leto clutched the trunk of a palm tree near the erect summit of Mount Cynthus and along the banks of the river Inopus. When he emerged from his mother's womb a golden hue brightened the land like soft sunlight and velvety blooms sprouted from the parched island soil. The newborn drank ambrosia and nectar from Thetis, precociously played the lyre and took up his ever present bow.

General view of the wide expanse of ruins on Delos

The harbor at Delos

The legend is that Apollo raised an altar to himself with the horns of goats slain by his arrows. He left the altar to Delos as a symbol of his gratitude and as a pledge of his love. Throughout antiquity Delos remained one of the most revered and cherished sanctuaries.

The worship of Apollo began at an early period, probably following the decline of the Mycenaean world and is believed to have been adopted from Crete.

By about 1000 B.C. Delos had become a refined and impressive cultural, religious and commercial mecca which eclipsed the adjacent circle of Aegean islands. All Greeks, all Ionians of Greece and Asia, the Dorians of Crete and the Peloponnesus, made regular pilgrimages to Delos. The harbor admitted a continual parade of vessels. Foreign visitors, whose ships brought precious unknown products, spilled onto the island from the busy harbor and headed straight for the temple of Apollo. Delos was sustained and enriched by the profits of commerce and by the pious offerings which the ancient world sent Apollo. In the streets of the spirited noisy town, one sacred procession after another wound its way to the temple to pay homage to the venerated god.

Delos became such a sacred place that it needed no fortification. Its sentry was Apollo. Even when the treasury of the first Athenian League was located there from 478 through 456 B.C., before it was transferred to the Acropolis, and vast stores of gold and precious gifts were lodged there, it remained unguarded and untouched. No Greek and no intruder would violate the sanctity of Delos during the centuries when Apollo worship was in its prime. Even the iconoclastic Persians who ruthlessly ravaged the temples of other gods, respected and did not plunder the temple of Apollo. All that Delos became, all that she acquired, her wealth, her impregnable security, her commercial and religious power, flowed from the influence of Apollo.

Around 540 B.C. the Athenians purged the island and removed all graves visible from the temple and moved them out of sight. Then, in the winter of 426 B.C., the Athenians cleansed Delos a second time, presumedly to prevent further pestilence and plague

The Sacred Way

Marble entrance to the inn

The commemorative palm tree

The ascent to Mount Cynthus, the only rise in the island

such as the Peloponnesian War. The island was deemed sacred and considered so spiritually chaste that no birth and no death could take place there. Dogs were prohibited because they could kill cats, rabbits and other animals and thus desecrate the hallowed island. All grave sites on Delos were exhumed and the bones and the burial gifts were removed to a communal grave, the purification pit, on the neighboring island of Reneia. Vases excavated from this pit are now in the museum in Myconos.

During the years of its glory Delos was virtually overlaid with sanctuaries. Devout pilgrims arrived at the ancient harbor which was centered on the west coast and guarded, as now, by two rocks, megalos and mikros Rematiaris, in the channel separating Delos from Reneia. They disembarked just below a high ancient wall overlooking the sea and adjacent to a low flat terrace which extended from the western perimeter of the area around Apollo's temple. A wall of granite rose perpendicularly from the sea and ran eastward. Behind Apollo's temple was another wall exactly similar, built of expertly contoured stone. To the north stretched a series of porticos whose inner walls served as another and complete enclosure.

Visitors paraded on the processional way past the terrace of marble lions, probably the best known statues on Delos. These lions were erected by the Naxians in the seventh century B.C. and it is believed that there may have been as many as sixteen at one time. Five lions now remain in Delos and a sixth headless one was removed to Italy and now guards the Arsenal in Venice. The lean elongated lions take on the form of stylized sea lions. Their heads face east, toward the Sacred Lake, the place where Apollo was born. Since 1925 the lake has been dry and in that place, and in remembrance of the god, a lone palm tree now stands.

As the pilgrims moved from the harbor to the temple the resonant sounds of chanting blended with the rhythmic cadence of the sea. The strong smell of incense sweetend the air and mixed with the fetid odor of sacrifial animals. The unremitting beat of the sacred choral dance drummed like a constant throb in the background.

The trading or commercial quarter of town was located to the north and south of the sacred area and along the western coast. The docks, warehouses and offices of the foreign trading companies were situated there. On the slopes of Mount Cynthus and overlooking Apollo's temple and the sea, rose the shiny white homes and temples to the foreign gods. Their bleached walls were partially obscured by the tall trees of the sloped woodland and reflected the sun in spears of fiery light.

In the harbor the visitors were welcomed on an expansive landing place decorated with highly wrought statues, porticos and platforms with benches to accomodate lively conversation. A wide opening on one side conveniently led to the commercial quarter. Three main arteries of the town originated here. One street led north toward the marketplace. One headed east following the outer walls of the temple area and led to the northern entrance. A third road traveled south and led to a secondary entrance to the sanctuary area, behind the harbor terrace.

Ancient excavated ruins on the abandoned sacred island

On each side of the sacred enclosure there were gates and pathways, some of which led to the upper slope area and others to the places of commerce. The main entrance to the temple, as was characteristic of Hellenic temples, was on the south side, to the right of the harbor and the busy quays.

The south or main entrance was adorned with the Propylaea or marble gateway built by the Athenians in the middle of the second century B.C. The road which led from the Propylaea and away from the temple is still clearly marked with the fragmented bases of marble statues which once lined the Sacred Way.

The open area in front of the temple was the most habitually frequented space. Gifts and offerings to Apollo were displayed there and the public books and records of the temple and of the town were stored there.

Entry through the Propylaea led to the heart of the main sanctuary. This area was filled with many structures, but one of the oldest and most significant buildings was the House of the Naxians. It was built in the seventh century B.C. and was dedicated to Apollo by the Naxians. It was long and narrow and had walls of granite. Eight marble columns divided the space and created two outer aisles. Just outside the north wall is the colossal base where the statue of Apollo once stood.

The temple of Apollo was crammed with dedications and relics. Offerings were placed on interior walls, on shelves and on tables, in chests and large ornamented containers. The offerings included Agamemnon's tiller, Leonidas's helmet from Thermopylae, Eriphyle's necklace and the bejeweled and ivory dagger of Darius's generals.

Each year an itemized list of these offerings was catalogued by the appointed officials of the sanctuary, the *hieropoioi,* and the list was inscribed in stone. A portion of the list from one such stone states: "... It received the following items in the temple of Apollo ... a gold signet, with an image of Apollo in carnelian, which Stratonike dedicated to Leto: weight 10 drs.; a gold necklace set with precious stones, which Stratonike dedicated to Leto, comprising 48

The terrace of the lions on Delos

The stylized lions face the now dry Sacred Lake

shield-shaped disks, and one in two halves, and one on either side of the central piece, and 141 pendants: weight 106 drs.; ...3 gold coins of Philip; 1 of Alexander; coins from various places: weight 68 drs.; a gold drinking cup, dedication of Echenike: weight 49 drs. 3 ob.; ... a gold crown of bay leaves, dedication of King Demetrius: weight 71 drs. 3 obs.; a gold crown of bay leaves, dedication of Polykleitos: weight 65 drs. 3 obs ..."

The temple of Apollo was not only a renown shrine, it was also an early financial conglomerate. It collected treasures for the god, it collected taxes and rents for the government of Delos, it loaned money at ten per cent interest and it supervised the expenditures for public works. Religion and commerce coexisted and prospered. The accounts of all of these transactions have been preserved in stone.

An illustration of the inscription regarding debts paid is as follows: "... and on behalf of Euthytime daughter of Diodotos, the in-

Close view of one of the lions on Delos

View of the Sacred Way

Ancient pottery on Delos

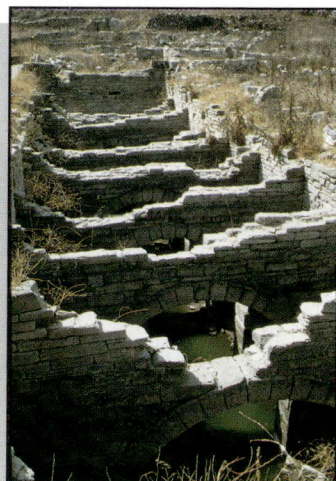

Cistern of the Theatre

Stoibadeion

terest he said he owed on the sacred money for the year of Demares, 39 drs 1 1/2 ob. From Aristoboulos son of Aristoboulos, on behalf of Orthokles son of Orthokles, the interest, arising from the guarantee made for the sacred money, which he said he owed on the sacred money, 101 drs. 3 ob ..."

Deliquent debtors were also publicly identified: "... Euphranor and his guarantor Aristeides son of Aristeides, the amount he did not pay for rent on the sacred 'Episthenes' house ... and 24 drs. 2/3 ob.; and Dionysodoros son of Marathonios and his guarantor Demeas son of Phokritos, the amount he did not pay for the ferrytoll to Rheneia, 62 drs.; and Antigonos son of Charistias, the amount he did not pay for the harbor tax ..."

The wealth of the sanctuary included houses and farm land which the officials of the temple confiscated from religious offenders. These properties were then rented to tenants and the income they generated increased the sacred treasury.

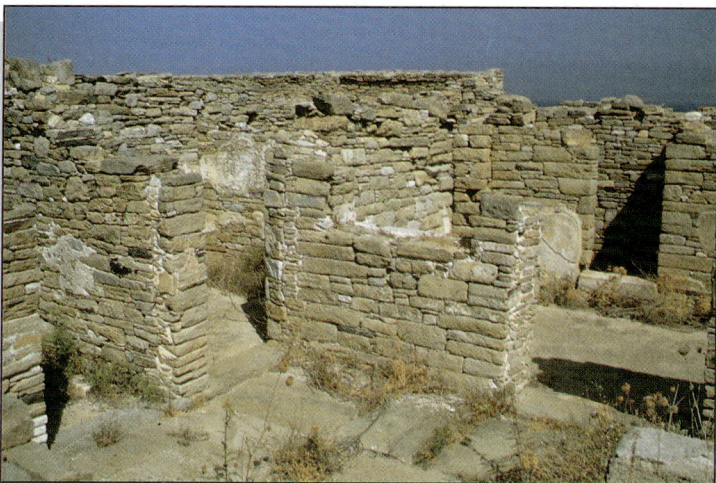

Ruins of ancient house on Delos

Beyond the sanctuary area was the commercial district. Egyptians, Syrians, Phoenicians, Palestinians, Jews and Romans arrived with ships laden with goods and slaves and traded and prospered there. They formed powerful guilds and established clubs which became meeting places for those of the same national origin. It was estimated that at one time nearly 10,000 slaves might change hands in a day in Delos.

The prosperity of Delos is evidenced by the high inflation expressed in the inscriptions. House rents soared steadily. Rich merchants would buy a block of homes then tear them down and remake them with more lavish replacements. Courtyards and peristyles would be enlarged, colonnades would be added and floors would be carpeted with intricate and impressive mosaics. The enterprising owner would then double or triple the rent.

One example of an especially sumptuous property is the House of the Masks which was discovered in 1939. It has been suggested that it may have been a luxurious inn for actors. It had nineteen rooms, including four which were decorated in mosaics. The house was named after one of the mosaics that depicted various theatrical expressions with the faces or masks of actors. The house had toilets, slave quarters and sunken terra cotta baths.

For generations Apollo inspired reverential prayer and commercial enterprise on Delos. But because of the playful nature of the god, he also aroused a contagious spirit of play and tough competition. It was not the brutal and bloody play of the Romans. Rather it was spirited, sensual play. Athletics, dance and song were an integral part of Apollo worship and periodic festivals were held in his honor. We may not know if indeed the first prize for an athletic competition was "a blameless accomplished woman and a tripod with handles" or for a boxing match "a six year old mule" as reported in the *Iliad,* but we do know that the festivals included women, unlike the festivals at Olympia which excluded women on penalty of death.

The *Odyssey* makes reference to Apollo and to the annual festival in his honor, the Delia, which dates back to the eighth century B.C.:

"Many are your temples and wooded groves:
All peaks, lofty cliffs of high mountains
Are dear to you, and rivers flowing into the sea, Apollo;
yet in Delos does your heart take most delight,
Where the long-robed Ionians gather in your honor
With their children and modest wives.
Remembering you they give you pleasure
With boxing and dancing and song ...
A man would say that they are immortal and age not
If he came upon the Ionians at this gathering;
For he would see the grace of them all,
And rejoice in his heart at the men
And women with their fine figures,
And their swift ships and many possessions."

Delos reveled in the memory of Apollo. The joyous spring festivals were held to commemorate his fortuitous birth there. Pretty

Ancient fallen columns on Delos

The theatre at Delos

House of Dionysos

young women, daughters of the most prominent Delian and Athenian families, dressed in their finery, wore wreaths of wild flowers and sang and danced around Apollo's altar. In sinewy steps they expressed in dance how Leto had wandered throughout the world, how she had come to Delos with child and how Apollo was born. Twelve animals were taken each year to Delos for sacrifice. These ancient rituals created a sense of awe and induced an atmosphere of holiness.

Garlands were festively hung on the many island statues. Choruses of young men and women chanted the familiar sacred hymns and expertly performed the *geranos,* an ancient dance of twists and turns that simulated pathways in the labyrinth at the Palace of Minos at Knossos. It is believed that Theseus stopped at Delos and danced at the altar of Apollo when he fled Crete after slaying the Minotaur. He is credited with the founding of the Delian Games and the selection of the palm frond as the treasured first prize for the winner.

In addition to the annual spring festival, another more elaborate festival was held every five years and was instituted by the Athenians. All Ionian cities participated. From all over Greece, from the surrounding islands and from as far away as Asia, sacred representatives, *theoria,* were sent as emissaries to the festival. These emissaries were transported to Delos in a galley filled with fragrant spring flowers and manned by a crew of free men. Delos was declared morally pure when the galley set sail. The priests from the temple invoked a divine blessing and decreed that the island could not be defiled by any death sentence until the return of the galley to Delos.

The festival officially opened when the sacred representatives arrived. They disembarked in the harbor amid applauding crowds. On occasion impatient spectators pushed prematurely forward, overwhelming the ambassadors before they were dressed in their ceremonial robes and symbolic garlands of flowers. Often, to avoid the restless throng, the sacred group went to the small companion islet opposite Delos to prepare, then landed in full regalia on Delos.

During one particular year, Nicias, an Athenian general of the fifth century and one of the most devout men of his time, prepared an especially memorable spectacle.

In his ship from Athens, Nicias transported an enormous bronze palm tree which thereafter stood near the statue of Apollo and a disassembled wooden bridge which had been ornamented with thin layers of gold, painted figures and fine tapestries. In the darkness of night, on the eve of the Pan-Ionic festival, his crew assembled the pontoon bridge then threw it across the narrow channel which separated Delos from Reneia. In the morning the spectators marveled at the unexpected sight.

The sacred procession of Athenians, slowly and with great stateliness, wound over the gilded bridge. Musicians whose festive costumes glittered in the warm spring sun filled the air with songs of praise. The smell of sacrifice and incense hung heavily on the moving throng. Choruses chanted reverent hymns. Others regally carried a steady stream of offerings destined for the irrepressible god. The procession was officially received at the opposite end of the bridge by an appointed representative from Delos who formally greeted the pious group. The group then made its way to the temple to present its offerings and prayers to Apollo. Several days of celebration and competition followed.

Apollo is gone now. The pagan god has long been overthrown. The Delian festivals ceased in 316 B.C. The marble statues, the sacred altar, the temple itself have been ravaged by seamen in search of ballast, by lime burners who calcined the precious marble and by Turkish plunderers whose marble tombstones on adjacent islands were cut from the remains of Delian temples. During the Ottoman occupation, the bronze cramps which held the joints of the buildings together were also looted and became valuable acquisitions at a time when metal was scarce. The island had also been raped by the provveditore of Tinos who severed the Collosus of Apollo in his thieving efforts to remove it from Greece to Venice. Even halved, it was too heavy to ever leave the island.

In the sixth century B.C. the Naxians had erected the colossal sta-

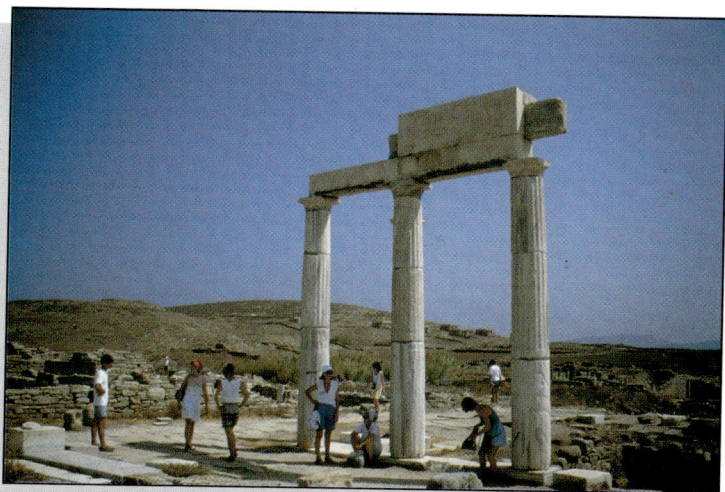

Columns from the building of the Poseidoniasts

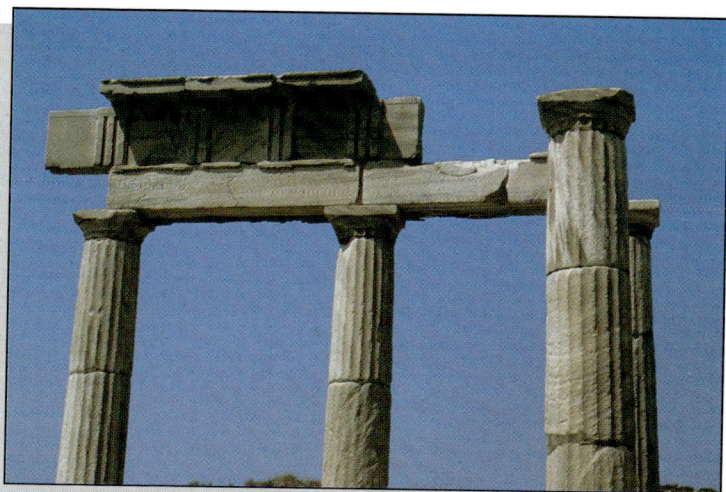

Detail from the building of the Poseidoniasts on Delos

Mosaic floor from ancient house in the Theatre Quarter

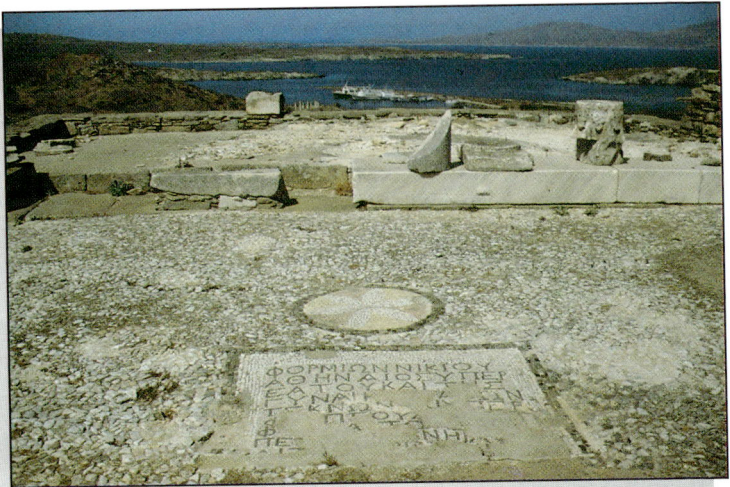

Patterned mosaic floor from ancient home

The abundant traces of the ancient past

Agora of the Compitaliasts

tue of Apollo which was four times life size. He was depicted in the rigid *kouros* style, a slender nude male facing front, one foot forward, arms at his sides with elbows bent and fists clenched. Additional metal parts have been found, long curls from the head and a belt for the waspish waist. The sculpture was positioned on a large base which contained the inscription, "I am of the same marble, both statue and base."

The most catastrophic pillaging of the island, however, took place in 87 B.C. when Menophanes, one of the generals of Mithridates, demolished the temples of Delos, threw the statues into the Aegean and massacred and enslaved the population. It was a tragedy from which Delos never finally recovered. Delos ceased to be regarded as a commercial or holy center. In the first centuries of the Christian era, the Athenians offered the island for sale. There were no buyers. Ultimately Delos was acquired by Mykonos. They leased the land for pasture and grazing to a handful of shepherds who lived on the land. Delos became known as Small Delos and Reneia which has more cultivable land and is inhabited by modern Delians is known as Great Delos.

Today Delos is a desolate place. There are no hostelries, no quayside restaurants, no grand agora and no annual spring festival. The hot noon sun lays leaden on the island's features and flattens them, leaving no shadows to soften the angular decaying ruins. As far as the eye can see there is a panorama of ancient stone.

Delos is level but for the promontory of Cynthus, centered in granite, which has an arresting view of Delos and the sea. The summit is not especially high, but it stands in marked contrast to the low hills and flat plain. Delos is a mere skeleton of what it once was. The silence is periodically broken by the metal clank of archaeologists' tools or by the multilingual chatter of tourists. A solid thread of tourists moves from the quay to Mount Cynthus then unravels through the maze of grey ruins on the floors of abandoned Delian homes. These transitory guests arrive in boatloads from Mykonos and Paros, not to pay homage to Apollo, not to barter for wheat or corn or slaves in the marketplace, but to rake through the residue

Remains of statue of Cleopatra

of one of the most powerful centers in the Aegean. The seasonal pilgrims are inspired by a leisurely interest in antiquities and by a desire to pass the summer afternoon on a cool and pleasant sea excursion.

Delos is unquestionably the most varied archaeological site in the Aegean and although it is the most ravaged, it is nevertheless regarded by scholars as an ideal site to train students in archaeology. It is the smallest and most central of the Cyclades. It is a thumb-shaped strip of metamorphic rock and granite that is nearly devoid of vegetation. Occasional clusters of wild red poppies sprout from the marble bases and bring new life and color to the caked infertile soil.

Delos is about halfway between mainland Greece and Crete to the south, and Samos, Cos and Rhodes to the east. Inevitably, by virtue of its advantageous location, it became a main intersection for maritime commerce. All the great trade routes converged there. Traders from Palestine and Syria, from Italy and the Black Sea routinely sold slaves, exchanged goods and worshipped Apollo with equal intensity.

The original temple built for Apollo was quite simple. In the early fourth century B.C. Athens replaced it with another less primitive temple. It was constructed entirely of Parian marble and was small but clean and beautiful in its proportions and in its simplicity. It had plain unfluted Doric columns with intriguing sculptures on the pediment. The temple was scaled down to correspond to the use for which it was intended. It was exclusively designed for Apollo as his sole private refuge. Only the priests and a few magistrates had access. It was not the place where worshippers flocked to offer prayers and sacrifice. The place of worship was limited to the sacrificial altar, the open space outside the confines of the temple.

The sacred compound enclosed the temple as well as all the other structures consecrated to Apollo. The sacrosanct area was surrounded by an enclosed wall known as the *peribolos* or *temenos*.

Within the sacred enclosure there were two smaller temples built at a later time. One was dedicated to Leto and one to Aphrodite.

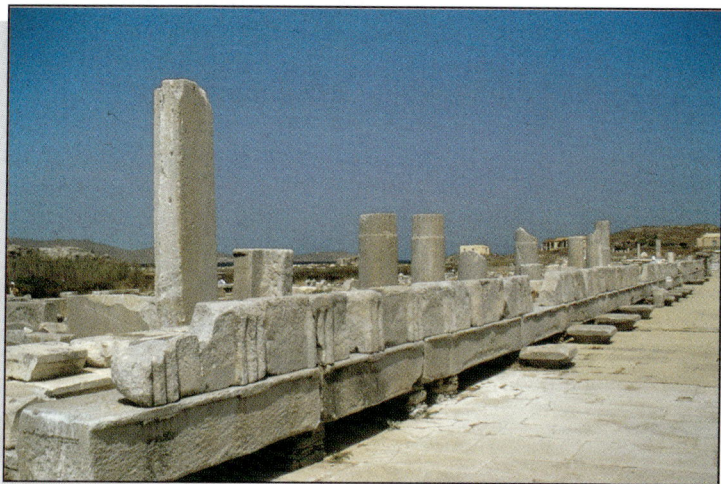

Sacred Way from the south

The ruins from the Domestic Quarter

There were treasuries and refectories and spacious porticos where priests offered lodging to the visiting worshippers. This tradition of hospitality was characteristic of most Hellenic sanctuaries and is regarded by Greeks as one of their distinguishing virtues.

Alongside Apollo was an altar for his twin sister Artemis. There were two temples to honor her, the Temple of the Seven Statues, the more ancient, and another called the New Artemisium.

Other gods were also worshipped in the enclosure. There was an altar for Zeus Polieus and others for Dionysus and Asclepius. Other buildings in the complex included the tomb of the Hyperborean virgins and closer to Apollo's temple, the dwelling of the priests or *neocorion.*

When paganism died Delos fell. Its prosperity had been artificial. It was too small and too infertile and too dry to support a population absent the alluring attraction of Apollo. The craggy island died.

The archaeological excavations on Delos have uncovered countless ancient treasures. The digging continues today. In 1872 the French Archaeological School began their work. Initially when they focused on Delos several papers were written about the history of the island but nothing more was pursued. It was not until the soil itself was analyzed that the actual work commenced. The most vexing problem was precisely where on the island the first spade should enter.

M. Lebeque led the excavations in 1873. He directed his attention to the summit of Mount Cynthus and discovered a curious shrine and two temples. Unfortunately he neglected the littoral area which was shaped by the ancient coast. When he departed the Archaeological Society at Athens continued the work on Delos and discovered the shrines of the foreign gods, Serapis, Isis and Anubis, on the slope of the summit.

In 1877 Albert Dumont resumed the excavations. He appointed M. Homolle to superintend the work. His years at Delos were fruitful and productive.

The character of an ancient site dictates the point of attack and determines the method of excavation. Delos had been a religious and commercial center and hence the sanctuary area and the commercial quarter correctly became the focal points of Homolle's search.

Imperfectly defined pillars were just visible from the soil along the west coast. There were the traces of the vast warehouses which housed the products from foreign traders. The original plan was to unearth that area, to reconstruct the harbor, the quays and the docks and to reveal the town plan of Delos.

It was recognized that this plan was not without some risk. The danger was that the commercial center would be uncovered at the expense perhaps of the temple of Apollo.

Locating the general area of the temple was relatively simple. It could only be on the one plain available for the construction of large buildings, the expansive ground from the foot of the summit to the coast. And on the plain surrounding the temple the comple-

The evidence of many periods, one atop the other

mentary buildings and temples must be located.

What was difficult was to determine precisely where on this plain the temple was placed. Nothing emerged from the soil to give direction. Not one building remained standing. Not even a vague outline of a building existed.

Under the heavy weight of the rock-hard soil a few structures seemed scattered around the Sacred Lake and along the western shore. Then, toward the center of the plain a large parallelogram appeared. Two parallel lines of ruins extended from it. On one side a vast rectagular structure was discerned and then bases of scattered statues emerged.

Unfortunately there had been no ancient guides to focus the work. Pausanias did not visit Delos. And the eight books written by Semes, himself a Delian, which described the island and its workings in great detail were irretrievably lost.

Aristotle's treatise on the Republic of the Delians was also lost. It too would have suggested the plan and assisted the dig. Lost also were the ancient poems which celebrated the island's traditions and which we learned about from the references in the inscription which were ultimately found.

The excavations, then, were begun without direction. As a result, they were initially accompanied by a strong sense of pessimism and concern. The most that the French hoped to find were tangible facts necessary to restore the structures and inscriptions needed to fill in the details. After the parallelogram had been sighted they found the foundation to the temple. From then on they continued to discover reliable data. The archaeologists led an ascetic austere life, endured bouts of fever and were seemingly oblivious to the isolation. They remained on the island for more than five months at a time directing groups of up to 200 workers, measuring, reconstructing, restoring, cataloging, deciphering and drawing plans. Their efforts are evidenced on Delos today. Between 1904 and 1914 many ancient buildings were found, including the sanctuary of Apollo and a large part of the old town.

A visit to Delos today can be overwhelming. There is so much that has been unearthed that it confuses the untrained eye and the centuries run together as one. The sheer volume and variety of antiquities can deaden, for a time, sensate impressions. To ease the exploration of the island most guidebooks divide the ruins into four digestible quarters and recommend taking in each section slowly and with some guidance: the sanctuary of Apollo, the residential neighborhoods, the commercial quarter and the temples of the foreign gods.

While each area contributed significantly to the history of Delos, the residential section is of particular interest because the homes are so well preserved and reveal so much of life in the second and first centuries B.C.

The heart of the home was the courtyard. Various rooms were arranged around the courtyard and the open court was their source of light and fresh air. The more extravagant homes had a peristyle with simple Doric columns. Large richly decorated halls served as

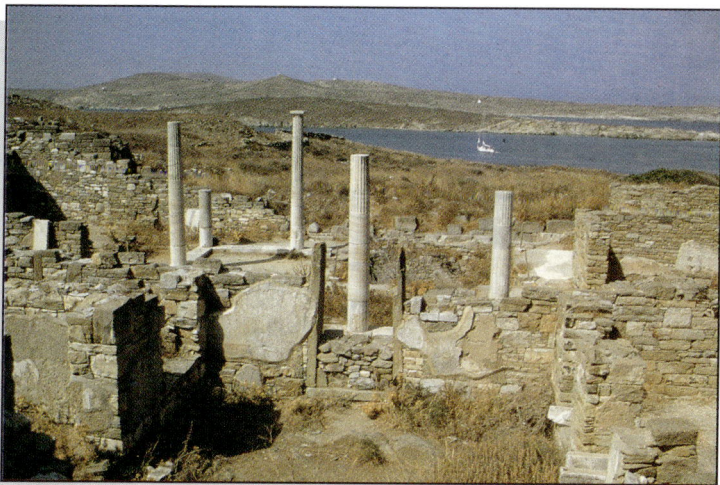

Ruins of an ancient home near the harbor

reception rooms where banquets might have been held. There were also toilets and baths. Most homes were on one level, but the grander residences had two or more stories. Fountains and cisterns were the water sources and they were built below ground level for practical and aesthetic reasons.

One of the most remarkable features of some of these homes is the floor covering. Courtyards and rooms were frequently decorated with mosaics of unique designs. Over 350 mosaics have been found on Delos and of that number well over 100 are of great artistic quality.

The mosaics of Delos are regarded as the best yet found from Hellenistic Greece. They are unusually well preserved because the population of Delos dropped dramatically before the end of the first century B.C. and by the seventh century A.D. the island was deserted.

Mosaics were not regarded as an art form in ancient times, probably because they were viewed primarily as utilitarian. They were easy to clean, resistant to water, did not have the foul smell of tamped earth and were highly decorative. Pliny has called them "a kind of painting in stone."

It is interesting to note that even the least known sculptor of that time signed the work, but the maker of the mosaic was nearly always anonymous. Only two mosaics are signed on Delos, one with a geometrical design in the Sanctuary of the Syrian Gods and the other in the House of the Dolphins.

The mosaics on Delos were composed of recycled waste such as chips of marble and potsherds. Marble was universally used on Delos at that time so sculptors produced large quantities of fragments that comprised an almost limitless supply for the mosaic workshops.

Mosaics were created by arranging individual pieces in a preconceived design on a bed of cement. The best works give the illusion that the pieces are blended into a harmony of line and surface. The critical design feature was usually the center. Around that radiated concentric designs and a border.

Many mosaics were obvious attempts to imitate painting. The ground was the canvas. In some cases the entire floor mosaic was removed from its original location and placed elsewhere. This was found to have happened at least eight times on Delos. This shows that the mosaic was treated more like a painting and was regarded as independent of the surrounding space.

The beauty of the temples, the harbor, the homes of Delos has survived. But an eerie silence pervades it all. Today Delos lives in its past. And for Delos the past is Apollo. In 1820 Shelley portrayed the power and the beauty of the virile god and immortalized him in a poetic hymn. It is as close as we will come to the inspiration for it all:

> "... I feel the clouds, the rainbows, and the flowers,
> With their etherial colors; the moon's globe,
> And the pure stars in their eternal bowers,
> Are cinctured with my power as with a robe;
> Whatever lamps on earth or heaven may shine
> Are portions of one power, which is mine.
> I am the eye with which the universe
> Beholds itself, and knows itself divine;
> All harmony of instrument or verse,
> All prophecy, all medicine, are mine,
> All light of Art or Nature; to my song
> Victory and praise in its own right belong."

View from Samos of the ever present sea

5

SAMOS

Samos and the sea are indivisible. No element has done more to mold the contours of her land and the character of her people than the moody mercurial Aegean. Thunderous then calm, capricious then constant, translucent then a menacing black, its ever-changing disposition shaped the Samian spirit and preordained her destiny.

Samos became an island milleniums ago when the earth shook so violently that it wrenched the fist-shaped mass of land from the coast of Asia Minor. The Straits of Mykali now separate it from the Turkish mainland.

The natural features of the small island closely resemble the Turkish coast. There is a continuity in the strong defined horizontal line in the mountains, in the configuration of the inlets and bays and even in the geology. Rocks of the Pliocene Age, perhaps five or six million years old, were found on Samos and are believed to be deposits from an ancient river, the Menander River, in Turkey.

The sea enticed the Samians and made them restless and enterprising. Each day from every hillside and headland they could see and smell the sparkling sapphire sea. Transfixed by their vision they dreamed of unknown lands, separated by the sea but linked in their reverie by the intervals of islands off in the distance. Icaria is a mere ten miles away. The massive Turkish mainland looms within view. They were naturally beckoned by what they saw and what they imagined they would find. They were seduced, made discontent, lured from their comforting sweet-smelling land by the tempting surrounding sea. Inescapably they became expert sailors and dauntless adventurers. They have been called the British of the Aegean.

From ancient times Samos produced generations of hardy mariners willing to risk what they knew they must. They learned to read cloud formations and to smell and sense the winds and to watch birds fly. Winds, they knew, heightened the dangers at sea.

They discovered that certain winds were predictable and the accurate anticipation of them reduced the inherent risks. The Birdwinds, for example, brought the birds of passage and blew in the spring from the north. In the summer from the same quarter the Etesian winds would come.

The Samians matured into highly proficient sailors who understood and tolerated the petulence of the sea. One of the most fearless Samian sailors was Koleos, the first to pass through the Pillars of Hercules, now Gibraltar, and sail into the Atlantic. Koleos returned to Samos with knowledge of the tides, with awareness of a greater world and with a deep fondness for Iberia.

The beauty of Samos is soft and subtle. The mountains are bold and clearly cut but with no jagged edges to make them harsh. The inclines are gentle and dignified. Wordsworth might have thought of Samos when he wrote of "the lively Grecian, in a land of hills." There is a sense of peace and symmetry, perhaps because the sea

The quaint beauty of an island home

The modern quay at Pythagorion

The seaside cafe lining the harbor at Pythagorion

Pythagorion harbor

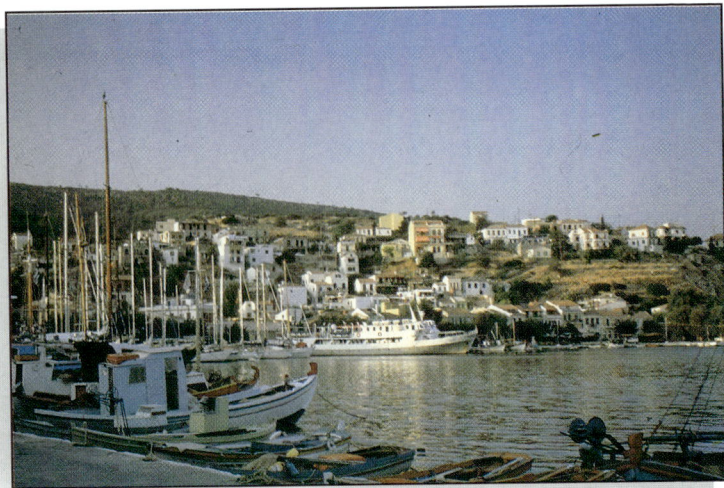

The modern port at Pythagorion

The sacred road which linked ancient Samos with the site of the Heraion

Entrance to the site of the Temple of Hera

commingles so harmoniously with the mountainous land.

Ancient Samos was heavily wooded and shaded in various hues of green. There were, as now, a wide variety of fruitbearing trees and shrubs. The pomegranate bush, which once grew wild, was introduced by the Phoenicians. The Phoenicians also brought the cypress trees which point upward like erect spires in the green hills. They originated from the highlands of Afghanistan and were first transported to Persia, where they became a spiritual symbol of fire worship, then to the temporate Mediterranean coast.

Anemones paint the hillsides with wild splotches of white, scarlet and purple. The blossoms nod in the gentle breeze like dainty cups of silk. According to some sources they symbolized the blood of Adonis. Others maintain that they were formed by the tears that Aphrodite shed for Adonis. On an early spring day clusters of ostentatious cyclamen, tall thin gladiolus and golden narcissus brighten the island soil and are as precious to the Samians as a harvest of grapes. On hilltops overlooking cultivated fields, violets and crocuses sprout from drier more solid soil.

Samos remains fertile and rich in olive trees and vineyards which produce the muscat wines. There are still many indigenous carob trees and at higher elevations, tenacious aromatic pines. A wide variety of shrubs thrive under the nurturing warmth of the Samian sun.

It was fated that the magic of the island would be discovered by others who ventured from their homes by sea. The first colonists were probably from neighboring Asia Minor. It is believed that they migrated west over vast expanses of arid land, then stopped by the edge of the sea. In the distance was an island, "spread like a shield upon the misty sea" and they were determined to reach it. These early primitive settlers were followed by waves of Mycenaeans who migrated at different times from scattered parts of Greece.

Samos received many celebrated guests. Socrates spent time there, reportedly as a respite from the troubles at home. Herodotus spent three years in exile there. And for a pair of imperial lovers

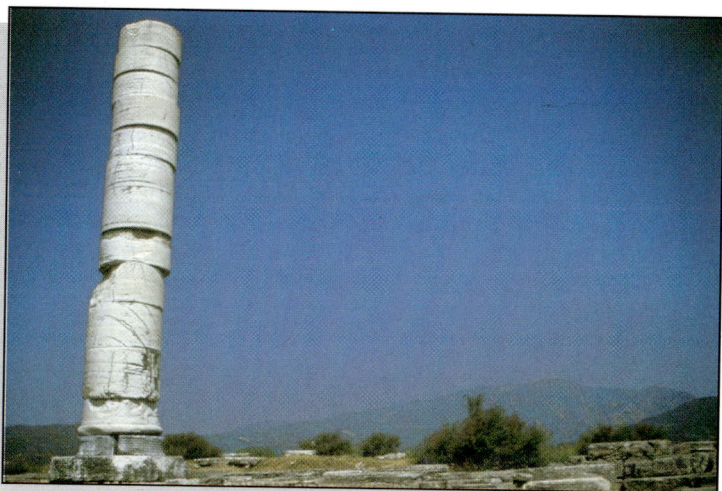

The sole surviving column from the temple built by Roikos in Polycrates' time

The ruins of the Temple of Hera

Samos was a treasured romantic retreat. Antony courted Cleopatra there. And if we adopt Plutarch's view, he haplessly fell victim to infatuation and threw away the world for the love of his queen.

Her burnished barge would rendezvous with his war galley in the ancient harbor that is now surrounded by the town of Pythagorion. Her lavishly ornamented vessel would glide in the harbor with fluttering deep purple sails and a stern of solid gold. A regiment of slaves, discreetly out of view, pulled oars of silver, inlaid with gold and ivory. As the oars rotated out of the sea they caught the fiery light of the sun and encircled the barge like a moveable fire.

The queen reposed on a wooden deck, richly carved and ornately gilded, and reclined on a sumptuous couch in a pavilion of silken gauze. A haze of dense perfume enclosed her and wafted smoothly from the barge to an adjacent wharf.

Young boys and girls pranced around her, fanning her and singing for her pleasure. An orchestra of flutes muffled the chants of the galley slaves and helped them keep the rhythmic stroke. Of her beauty, Shakespeare wrote:

> "Age cannot wither her, nor custom stale
> Her infinite variety: other women cloy
> The appetites they feed; but she makes hungry
> Where most she satisfies: for vilest things
> Become themselves in her; that the holy priests
> Bless her when she is riggish."

But Shakespeare could not resist a bawdy note even for the Egyptian queen:

> "Royal wench!
> She made great Caesar lay his sword to bed:
> He plough'd her, and she cropp'd."

With the exception of the immense harbor at Smyrna on the coast of Asia Minor, the ancient harbor at Samos was unrivaled. It was protected by an ancient mole that bounded the harbor, said to be twenty fathoms deep, and stretched like an elongated arm into the open sea. This extended arm gave the town its early name,

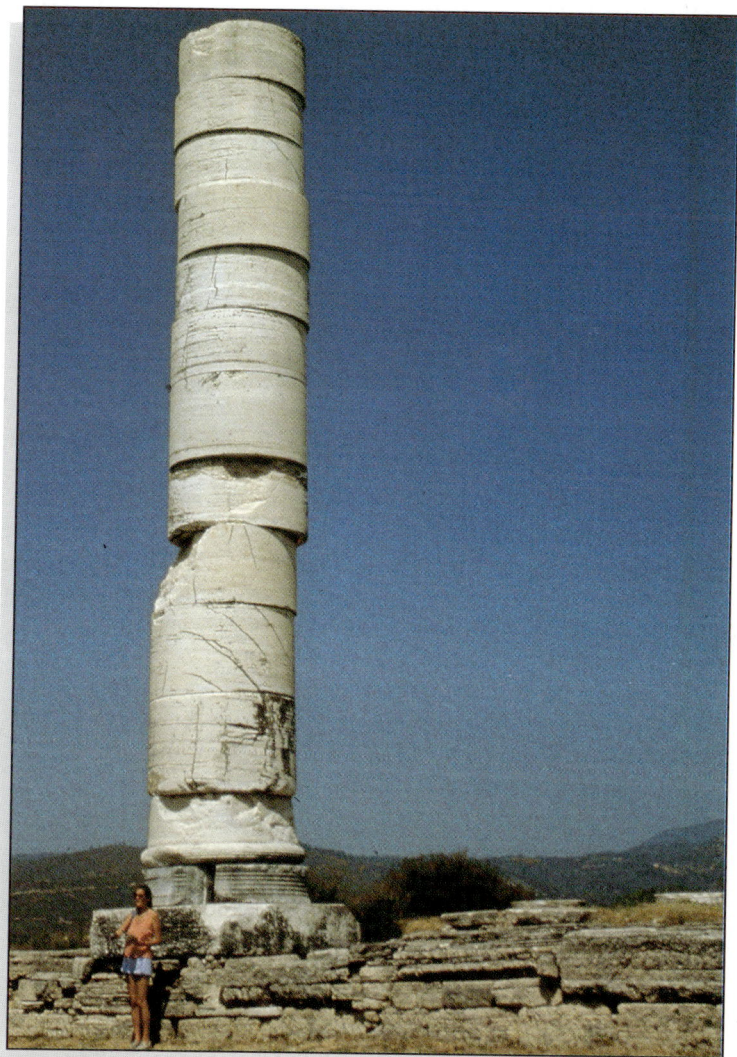

Last erect column with an adult in front of it to show its massive height

Tigani, meaning "frying pan". The long mole was the handle. The mole served the harbor as a breakwater. It was hailed by Herodotus as one of the greatest works in Greece in his time.

On one side of the harbor was an acropolis which may have been the site of a palace where the lovers stayed and where the ritualistic erotic feasts were held. It was one of the many places where the Egyptian loved her "demi-Atlas of this earth, the arm and burgonet of men."

The harbor mole was but one of the three great archaeological triumphs of early Samos and Herodotus extolled these great works in generous praise. Parts of each of them can still be seen in Samos today.

Herodotus wrote:

> "I have dwelt the longer on the affairs of the Samians, because three of the greatest works in all Greece were made by them. One is a tunnel, under a hill 150 fathoms high, carried entirely through the base of the hill, with a mouth at either end. The length of the cutting is seven furlongs, the height and width are each eight feet. Along the whole course there is a second cutting, twenty cubits deep and three feet broad, whereby water is brought, through pipes, from an abundant source into the city. The architect of this tunnel was Eupalinus, son of Naustrophus, a Megarian. Such is the first of their great works; the second is a mole in the sea, which goes all round the harbour, near twenty fathoms deep, and in length above two furlongs. The third is a temple; the largest of all the temples known to us whereas Rhoecus, son of Phileus, A Samian, was first architect."

These three achievements, the harbor mole, the tunnel of Eupalinus and the temple of Hera were completed during the era of Polycrates, around 550 B.C.

Polycrates was the first to conceive of a Greek empire with Samos at its center and with himself as despot. These feats have

The beautiful setting of the Heraion

View from the large altar of the Heraion

been described as monuments to his tyranny because of his autocratic rule. Polycrates was successful in maintaining power largely because of the incredible size and efficacy of his navy.

Most Greek warships at that time had a battering ram, a device that was mounted on the bow of warships. Polycrates designed a more sinister model, very long and tapered, intended not only to pierce the hull of an enemy ship, but also to open a way through the sea and hence increase speed. It was vaulted on the side attached to the ship to protect the deck from crashing waves. With elevated decks, unusual storage space in the holds for a greater supply of weapons and a menacing nose, these Samian ships appeared far more threatening than those of their enemy.

During the sixth century B.C. the naval fleet of Samos was widely known and feared throughout the Aegean. It was comprised of approximately 150 ships known as *samenae*. It was an immense fleet for its time. The fleet was used not only to vanquish opponents at sea, but also to extract tolls from foreign ships passing near Samos. The ships were also used to enforce mandatory protection payments from adjacent areas which benefited indirectly from the force and presence of the inimitable Samian fleet.

Polycrates also incorporated some triremes in his fleet. They were especially long vermilion ships, more narrow and limited in area than the customary warship of the time and manned by three banks of oarsmen or from fifty to over one hundred slaves. Samos was, after Corinth, among the first of the Greek naval powers to include the trireme in its fleet. Although it is believed that the legendary ship carried a full complement of ancient soldiers, it is unclear how a large number of troops could be transported on the long and shallow decks. Recently the Greek government sponsored the construction of a replica of the trireme by determined English scholars. The remarkable result of their collaborative five year effort bears a startling resemblance to the images of the slender ship on ancient vases and coins. With 170 oars in tight proximity the rowing is rigorously orchestrated to maintain the unison and to prevent the oars from overlapping. Nearly three thousand years after it first ap-

The setting of the ancient celebration of the Heraion, in honor of the marriage of Hera to Zeus

peared on the Aegean it has returned to sail in those familiar waters.

The uncanny good fortune of Polycrates was the subject of much serious deliberation and concern in his time. His life had never been disturbed by the normal vicissitudes of misfortune or loss. His friends cautioned that such immutable luck would inevitably provoke the wrath of the gods.

Amissis, the king of Egypt, sent an emissary to Polycrates with the message that he must create his own mishap before a more devastating event overtakes him. He warned his friend to guard against unrestrained happiness. Deprive yourself of your favorite woman he advised. Drink water instead of wine. Sink your best galley.

Polycrates heeded the advice halfheartedly. He studied the golden signet ring on his finger. It was set with a chunky emerald that was made by the noted Theodorus. This, he persuaded himself, is a sufficient deprivation. At the harbor he boarded one of his ships, ordered the captain to sail to the deepest waters and there he hurled the ring into the sea.

For three days he believed that he had appeased the gods. On the third day he was served a meal of fresh fish. In the stomach of the fish the emerald ring glowed.

The soothsayers warned Polycrates of the evil omen. The curse was now indelible. Amassis severed all ties with Polycrates because he knew the fateful end would soon come.

Polycrates prepared for potential ruin. His palace was guarded by about one thousand mercenary archers who kept their vigil on the acropolis overlooking the harbor with an unobstructed panoramic view.

Polycrates was ultimately destroyed by his own voracious greed. Determined to retrieve a treasure of gold that he was fooled into believing was real, he sailed from Samos and was killed by the barbarian who had deceived him. He was crucified on a wooden cross that was cruelly erected opposite Samos, so that in death Polycrates would always face the lush island he had thoughtlessly left behind.

During Polycrates' rule, from about 532 B.C., Samos flourished.

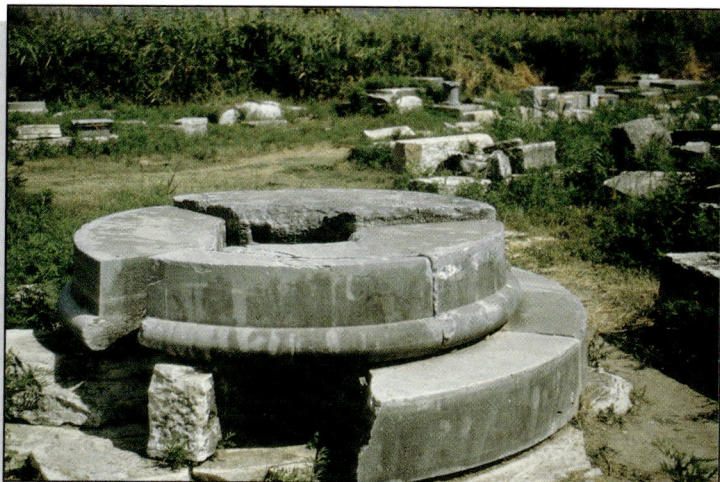

Massive pedestals at the Heraion

Fragments of excavated columns at the Heraion

Elegant detail from the ruins at the Heraion

Evidence of the massive columns that stood atop large circular bases

The excavation site at the Heraion

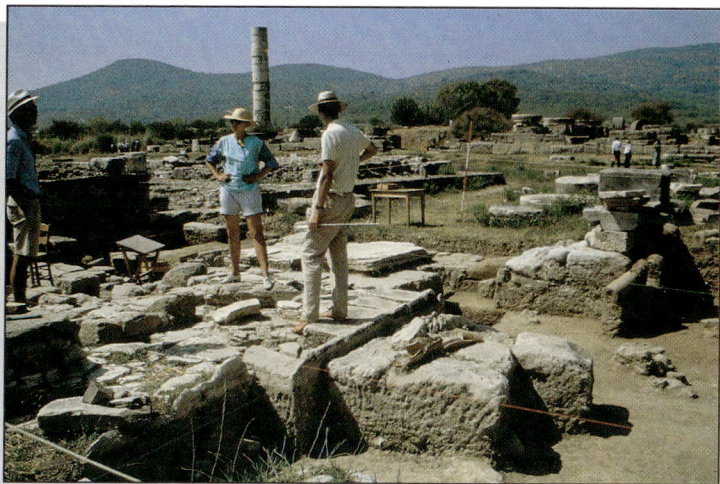

German archaeologist currently at work on the site

Some have urged that Polycrates was good for Samos at that time. He established a school of fine arts that became a standard of excellence for all Aegean art. And during his time he maintained the independence of Samos when Chios, Lesbos and other areas were subjugated by the Persians. Additionally, it was a thriving time when the famous harbor mole was built, the tunnel of Eupalinos was dug through the mountain and elaborate palaces and public buildings were constructed.

The tunnel of Eupalinos was described by Herodotus as the second major Samian feat. It was approximately 1000 feet long and was about eight feet in diameter. Parallel to the tunnel was a small tunnel used by the workers to repair leaks. It has been called the greatest engineering project of its time.

The tunnel or aqueduct was used to convey water from its source, the spring of Aghiades, to the town of Polycrates, now Pythagorion. It was also intended to conceal the precious water source from conquering enemies as it was channeled in earthenware pipes through the cavity carved inside the mountain.

In the centuries following its continued use in the sixth century B. C. the tunnel was oddly ignored and so thoroughly forgotten that successive generations were unaware of its existence. In 1883 a Greek Orthodox priest inadvertently rediscovered it. Archaeologists were then drawn to Samos to explore and reopen the passage. Earthen olive oil lamps were found in recessed areas periodically spread throughout the tunnel. The lamps were evidently used by the workers in the tunnel during the course of regular inspections and repairs. The workers stored their tools in convenient niches in the stone.

The tunnel was conceived by a hydraulic engineer from Megara, named Eupalinos, son of Nastroforus and it was completed with uncommon speed. Kastri, the mountain that rises in the northwestern part of the ancient city, was penetrated simultaneously from both ends. It was known then as the "double entrance tunnel". Hundreds of slaves began digging their way through solid rock with the aim of meeting precisely at the center.

Surviving pedestals of the missing columns at the Heraion

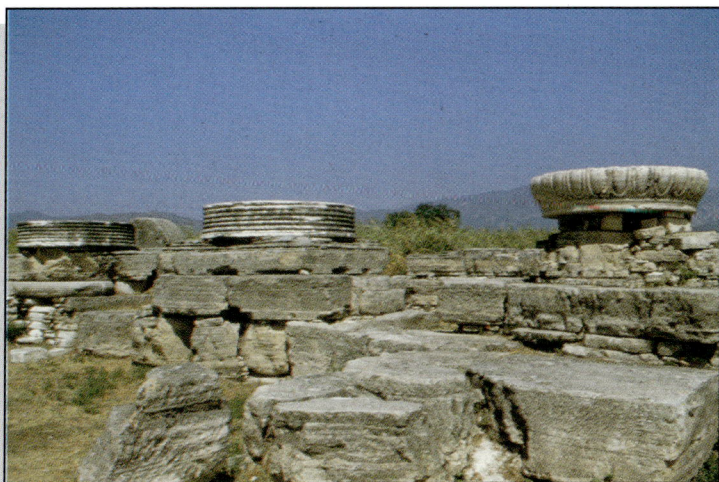

The massive bases of the ancient columns at the Temple of Hera

The excavation site at the Heraion

The sanctum of an old Christian basilica at the site of the Temple of Hera

Ancient relics at the Heraion

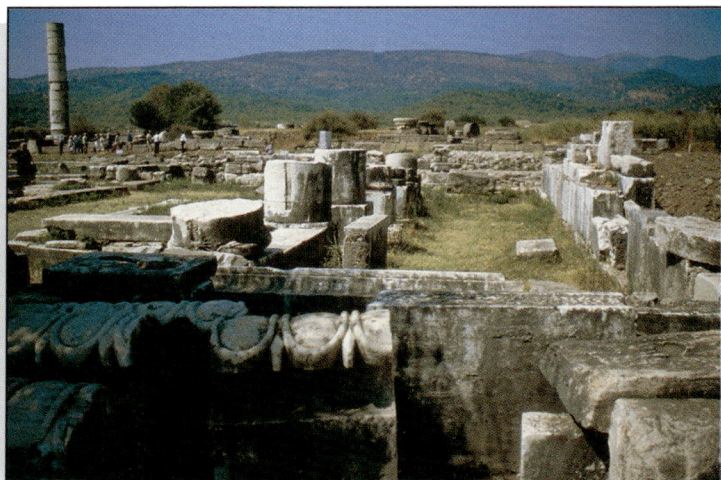

The excavated altar at the Heraion

The two camps of workers were composed of slaves, prisoners of war or victims of Samian raids who were under the continuous command of Eupalinos and the more immediate and stinging whip of their master. What is remarkable is that they nearly met in the middle, the deviation was a slight few feet, after slicing through the rock with primitive tools and pure brute strength.

The deviation was corrected by deepening and widening the northern end, which was somewhat higher than the southern side, until it connected in one uninterrupted channel. The southern exterior was found to be near the gate of an ancient building on the slope of Mount Kastri and adjacent to an ancient theatre. The northern opening was on the back slope of the mountain.

Polycrates built the tunnel for apparent security. He wanted to ensure that the city was regularly supplied with pure uncontaminated water and that its source did not fall into enemy hands. Polycrates knew that to make that source absolutely secure it had to be concealed. A stone reservoir was constructed over the water source, concealing it completely. A massive amount of earth was then placed over the reservoir. These protective measures preserved the reservoir through the centuries. In later years during the Christian era, a small chapel dedicated to St. John was built atop the camouflage over the reservoir. During the Turkish occupation the tunnel fell into oblivion until it was rediscovered in the late nineteenth century. Now it attracts summer tourists who climb the hill from Pythagorion to the tunnel in just minutes by motorbike or car.

It is ironic that such a small island could have inspired such oversized monuments, but the third great archaeological attraction on Samos and perhaps the greatest, is also distinguished by its size. The temple of Hera way well have been the largest temple in ancient Greece. Originally it had 133 columns. One alone now remains. It dwarfs each successive tourist who stands beside it for a photograph.

It was believed that Hera was born on Samos on the banks of the river that flowed adjacent to where the temple was built. The temple was placed on the site where she first coupled with Zeus.

Excavated ruins from the Heraion

In the sixth century B.C. the ancient architect Roikos designed and built the temple in an Ionic style. During the fifth century B.C. his son Theodoros rebuilt the temple after it had been burned by the Persians. It was approximately 354 feet long, over 164 feet wide and about 85 feet high. It contained so many works of art that it was respected as a great gallery.

The worship of Hera dated from prehistoric times. The original primitive altar was founded by the Nymphs and the Leleges. In the thirteenth century B.C. the first sovereign of Samos, Aghaios, built the earliest temple of unadorned wood and commissioned the first statue of the goddess for the simple sanctuary. The statue was an ordinary plank of wood crudely carved in the figure of the female deity.

In the era of Polycrates the temple was made more elegant and elaborate, a reflection of the prosperity and sophistication of that time. The columns were sculpted of lightly veined white marble with some pillars appearing to be an iridescent pale blue. The nave of the temple consisted of the portico and the sanctuary. There were two rows of immense Ionic columns. The portico was divided into three sections and in each section two towering rows of five marble columns stood tall.

A copper statue of Hera by the Samian artist Smilis was placed in the sacred interior. Another area of the sanctuary was adorned with a wooden figure of the goddess. She was depicted seated on a throne with an osier and two peacocks, her sacred symbols, at her feet. In still another part of the temple was a marble statue of Hera erect, a robe dropping aesthetically from her shoulders and a soft veil and gold diadem crowning her head. Regrettably this valued statue was taken to Istanbul where it was ultimately destroyed.

Offerings of great value were made to Hera. The rear portion of the temple was filled with statues of Zeus, Athena, Hercules and other heroes and gods. This area was described by Strabo as a great gallery. It was enclosed by a wall and within the enclosure were smaller temples dedicated to Aphrodite and others. Precious historical inscriptions and logbooks of famous Samian navigators

Ancient ruins found behind Temple of Hera

Ruins of a large ancient altar at the Heraion

were stored in *krators,* urnlike niches used as vaults for valuables.

The first reported person to see the temple of Hera in modern times was Joseph Tournefort, a French botanist and doctor, who went to Samos for scientific purposes in the early part of the eighteenth century. Tournefort saw the one remaining column as well as remnants of other columns and pedestals and did some minor excavations around the foundation of the temple.

Many efforts were made to conduct thorough excavations through the years but for one reason or another they were not pursued. In 1742 an Englishman named Ponnock visited the site and found that many of the marble remains had been destroyed or removed from the site. He sketched the first drawing of the sacred area which, it was later determined, was inaccurate. In 1812 the Society of Dilettanti of London sent scientists to Samos to study the ancient sites of Ionia. They conducted some minor excavations at the temple of Hera and made drawings of all the existing ruins at that time. Much of what they drew was missing when the next scientist, a German archaeologist named Ludwig Ross, examined the site in 1840.

In 1885 a French archaeologist, Victor Guerin, went to Samos. He was thwarted in his efforts to dig because of the unreasonable demands of the property owner whose vineyard covered the ancient antiquities and whose harvest of grapes was of greater importance to him than the old ruins beneath his fields. In 1860 Karl Humann, a German archaeologist, conducted some limited investigations and was the first to observe the more ancient ruins of Roikos beneath the remains of the later temple built by his son Theodoros. In 1870 the French archaeologist Paul Girard discovered a part of the foundation of the temple and exposed more ancient remains than all prior scientists.

In about 1902 the Archaeological Society of Athens attempted a new and complete excavation of the area at a time when the island was governed by Alexandros Mavrogenis. The funds, however, to support such an extensive dig were unavailable and the work was aborted.

In 1909 Theodor Bigand commenced new investigations pursuant to an agreement with the then ruler of Samos, Andreas Kopassis. The agreement permitted Bigand to remove some of the unearthed treasures to Berlin. In 1925 a new team of scholars began still another dig under the direction of Ernst Bruner of the German Archaeological Institute of Berlin. Bruner discovered two temples even older than the Roikos temple. After lengthy interruptions in the work during the 1940s, Bruner resumed the excavations in 1952 and continued to his death in 1961. Since that time the work has continued under new direction by the German Institute.

The temple of Hera was connected to the ancient capital city by an ancient sacred road. The road was constructed in the seventh century B.C. and was maintained through the Byzantine era. It was paved with slabs of marble and it was lined on both sides with elaborate buildings, temples, tombs and statues.

During the seventh and sixth centuries B.C. sacred processions passed from the city to the holy temples in honor of Hera. The two most celebrated events were the Heraia, commemorating the marriage of Hera and Zeus, and the Tonea which affirmed the innate power of Hera as manifested by the invincibility of her likeness. The people of Argos stole a wooden effigy of the goddess from the temple and tried to escape with it during the night. Hera's power forestalled their flight. In the morning they abandoned the statue on the shore and sailed from Samos empty-handed.

This small delightful island produced not only epic monuments but also gifted mathematicians, astronomers and philosophers including Aristarchos and Pythagoras, after whom the modern town was named. The most notable and endearing feature of Samos, however, is the constant sea. Now as in ancient times it is alternately tranquil and turbulent, distinctly blue and moody violet, but ever transcendent and timeless.

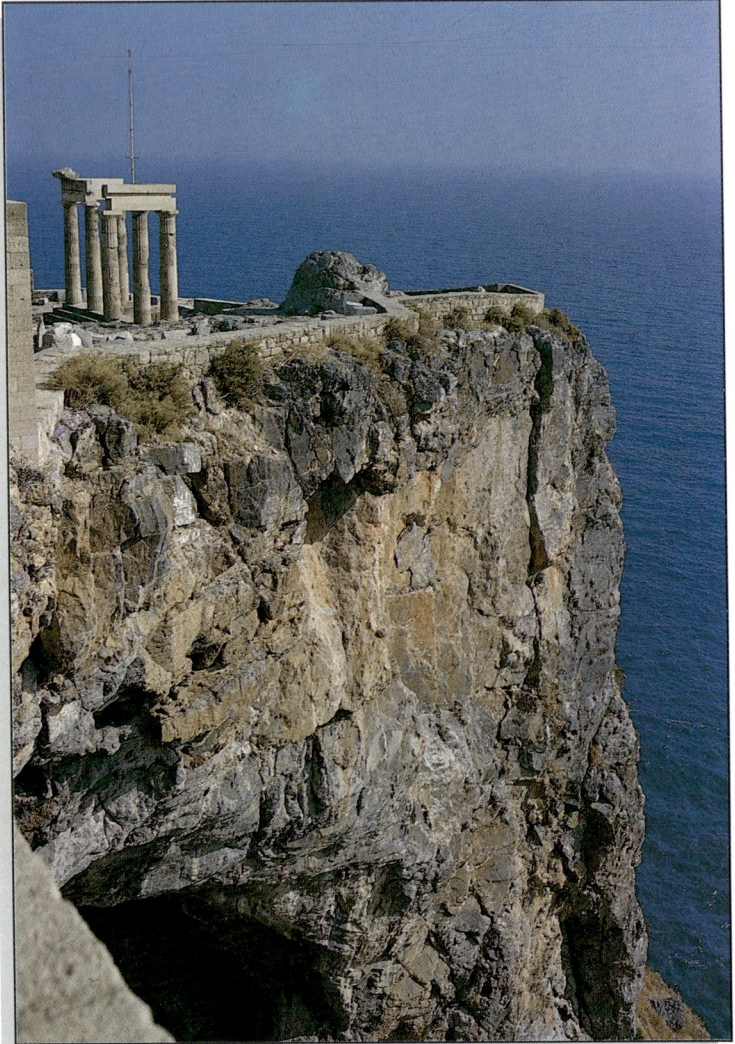

The acropolis of Lindos

6
LINDOS

The acropolis of Lindos soars like an assured sea bird ablaze in light gliding high above a dizzying precipice. From this exalted place the worship of pagan gods becomes infinitely more palatable. The enraptured expansive view takes in the unlimited sea and stretches across the unfettered Aegean to the bitten rock-hewn coast of Turkey. Two harbors lie on either side of the foot of the vertical promontory. One is a large unobstructed bay where ships appear as tiny miniatures afloat in a glittering tub. On the opposite side is a diminutive port with a pincer-shaped shoreline nearly enclosing the tiny day.

Like countless others, Lawrence Durrell was captivated by the startling beauty and elevation of Lindos. His memorable description evokes fathomable feelings of omnipotence and awe: "From the top of the cliff it looks like a peacock's tail spread out below - so brilliant and so various are its hues in sun and shadow. Your mind will say, 'Go on then, jump!' and for a long moment you will hover between the worlds of the dead and the living, hanging like a fly to the edge of the citadel."

It is here on this precipitous site in Lindos that the temple of the Lindian Athena was placed. The site was renown for its poised beauty and its insistence on chastity and purity. Strict rules regulated admission to the sanctuary and manifested ancient perceptions of human impurities. Women who had just made love, for example, and women who were menstruating or who had just lost their virginity were not admitted absent a purification bath. It is not surprising that these same rules did not apply to their corresponding male lovers.

All worshippers were required to enter the temple with clean bare feet. Only pure white shoes were permitted, provided they were not made of prohibitive horse's hair. Heads were covered. Weapons were forbidden.

The impressive coastline of Rhodes

Approaching Rhodes harbor

Rhodes harbor

The coast north of Lindos on Rhodes

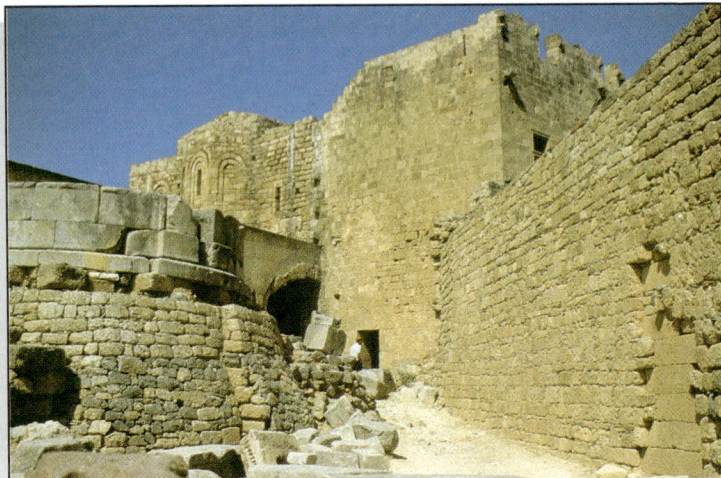

The way leading up to the entrance to the acropolis at Lindos

The mule ride up the acropolis

Lindos is situated on the eastern side of Rhodes, the remotest of the Aegean islands at the southernmost tip of the Archipelago. Rhodes is the third largest Greek island after Crete and Euboea and is one of the Dodecanese group. It is often warmly described as the island of roses.

Little is known of prehistoric Rhodes. The mythological accounts of the island appear to be ancient attempts to comprehend the unknown. Ironically, the myths closely parallel the known geological evolution of the island. Rhodes may not have risen from the bottom of the sea for the pleasure of the sun god, as Pindar recounts, but it was in fact the product of oceanic oscillations during the post-glacial period. Pindar's seventh Olympian Ode, composed in honor of Diagoras, a boxer from Rhodes, relates the history and mythology of Rhodes: "... The sun god could see a plot of land rising from the bottom of the foaming main, a plot that was destined to prove rich in substance for men, and kindly for pasture, and he

The rooftops of Lindos

urged that ... the island, when it had risen forth into the light of day, should forever after become a boon granted to himself alone ... From the waters of the sea arose an island ...''

The origin of the early island settlers is still in dispute. Thucydides reported that one of the first groups to invade Rhodes was the Carians, pirates who had come from deep within the interior of Asia Minor. It is presumed that they were followed by the Phoenicians who had come from the eastern Mediterranean. The Phoenicians resourcefully exploited the superb strategic and commercial position of Rhodes and wisely used it as a base of operations before continuing their migration west to Crete and beyond. Evidence of Phoenician artifacts was unearthed in Ialysos in northwestern Rhodes.

Since the period of the Trojan War, Rhodes had been divided into three major regions: Ialysos, located in northern Rhodes, Lindia, the largest region and located in the southern half of the island and Kamiros, the smallest area on the central western coast. Each region was regarded as a city-state with a separate administrative center. Lindos and Kamiros became town centers and Ialysos grew into a series of scattered but well-integrated settlements across the flat island plain.

Lindos prospered in Geometric times as a wealthy mercantile and naval city. It was ideally situated on the east coast and was naturally equipped with suitable harbors for ships traveling the Aegean. From the eighth to the sixth centuries B.C. Lindos flourished and grew into an important trading and ship-building center.

For about four decades during the sixth century, Kleoboulos governed Lindos and became famous throughout Greece as one of the Seven Sages. A rotund tomb with an interior rectagular burial chamber was found across the bay and to the north of Lindos. It is often referred to as the tomb of Kleoboulos but scholars remain unconvinced. The tomb has been converted into a Christian church of St. Aililianos.

Kleoboulos is credited with the rebuilding of the sanctuary of the Lindian Athena. The artful renovation of the temple regenerated

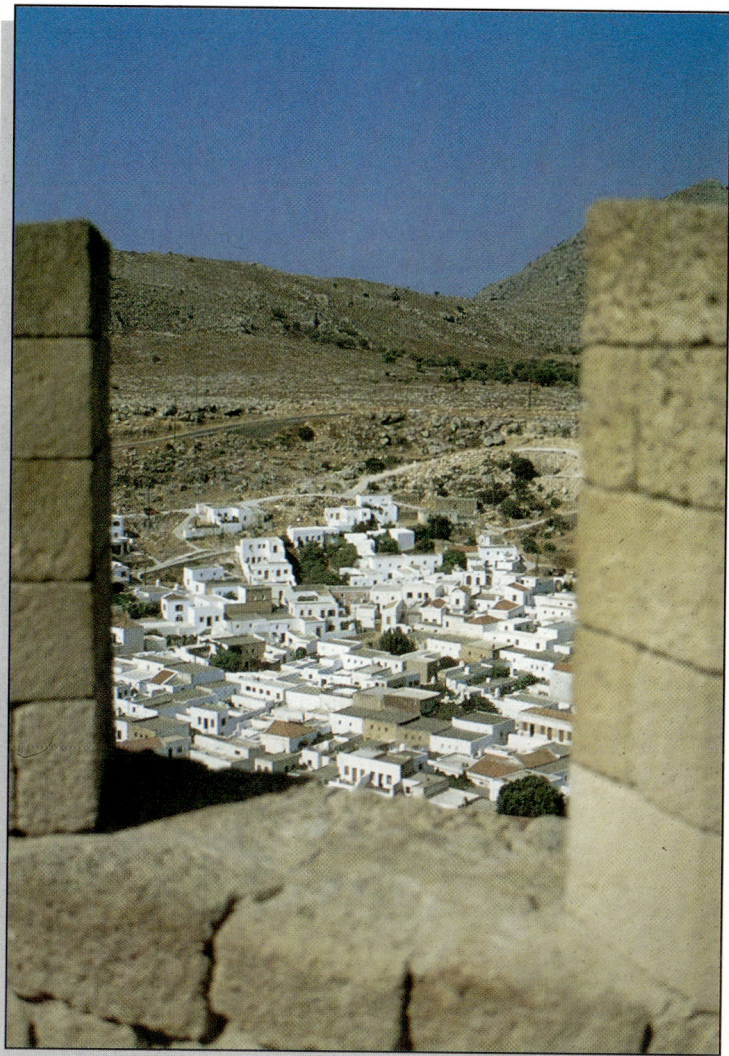

View of the town of Lindos atop the medieval castle

and perpetuated the cult of the goddess. Kleoboulos did for Athena what Polycrates did for Hera on Samos. Kleoboulos replaced the original temple with a grander one built on the imposing acme of the acropolis above a natural cave in the high steep cliff. The Doric temple stood like an illustrious jewel approximately 380 feet above the sea. He crowned the head of the primitive wooden statue in pure gold. In 342 B.C. the rebuilt temple and the statue were destroyed by fire. They were later rebuilt on the same site.

Unlike most men of his time, Kleoboulos believed, as did Pythagoras, that women should not be precluded from study or work. Among his students were his own wife and daughter. His daughter Cleobulina became a respected poet.

Few select but fascinating facts are known of Kleoboulos. His beauty was as celebrated as his prolific poetry. He wrote thousands of acrostics and other verse. He also wrote one of the most widely known and often quoted Greek epigrams, "Nothing in excess".

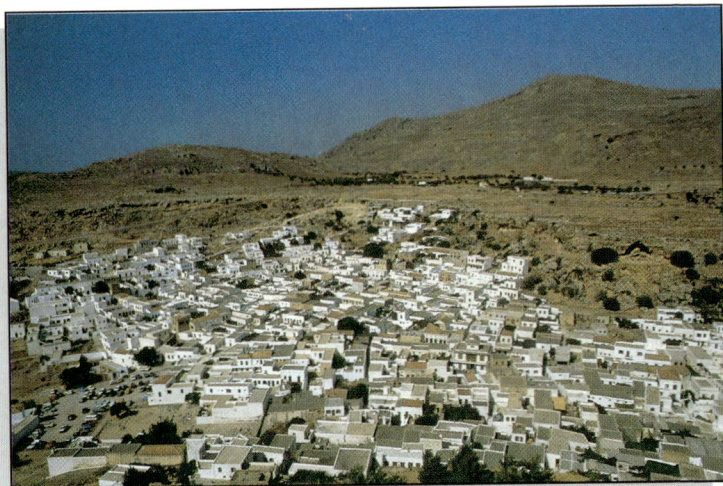

The flat roofs of the town of Lindos

The town seen from the acropolis

Kleoboulos was known to have been a close and loyal friend of So-
lon and when Peisistratus gained power in Athens he invited his
friend to Lindos for sanctuary. During his rule Lindos achieved a
remarkable level of sophistication. Even though Kleoboulos was in
fact a tyrant, he was regarded as a beloved tyrant to the common
populace in that he challenged and defied aristocratic rule.

Lindos, along with Ialysos and Kamiros co-existed harmoniously despite sharp fundamental political differences. Ialysos and
Kamiros were governed by the aristocracy while Kleoboulos ruled
Lindos. This incongruous accord was due in great part to the re-
mote geographical position of Rhodes and the sparsity of Karia, a
region opposite Rhodes on the coast of Asia Minor where small colonies were founded by Rhodians. Unlike the famous Karian cities
of Miletos, Ephesos and Smyrna, no such exceptional settlements
developed to overshadow Rhodian rule. Living far from the Greek
mainland and from other major centers made Rhodians more self-

One of the many lovely doorways in Lindos

Example of one of the many impressive doorways in the old town

sufficient and self-assured than they might otherwise have become.

In 408 Lindos, Ialysos and Kamiros united to found a capital city on the northern end of the island. The city too was named Rhodes. Despite successive incursions by Christians and Moslems it survives as the modern capital.

In 227 B.C. a devastating earthquake shattered the island and the Colossus of Rhodes was supposedly destroyed. The Colossus was a huge bronze statue of the sun god, over 100 feet high, and its creator, Chares of Lindos, worked for twelve years to complete it. The precise site of this enormous figure and indeed the fact of its existence remain unresolved. It is believed by some that it stood for over six decades before it shook and fell. Some urge that it actually straddled the harbor, but it appears that most statue fragments were found on land.

The statue ruins remained untouched until about 635 A.D. when the bronze pieces were confiscated by the Saracens and sold in the Levant. According to popular myth the sun god forbade restoration of the statue because of his deep displeasure with his postured image. A bit of Rhodian gossip exhorts, with some bitterness, that their Colossus was returned by the Turks piece by piece, remolded in the form of fiery bronze cannon balls when they invaded Rhodes in 1522.

Archaeological findings confirmed that Lindos thrived in Hellenistic times. In the sixth century B.C. Kamiros struck coins with the image of a fig leaf and traded primarily with settlements on the coast of Asia Minor and in the Aegean. Lindian trade, by contrast, was more cosmopolitan. The Lindians minted their own coins and used the Phoenician standard to facilitate transactions with them as well as with the Egyptians. Later, in the fifth century B.C., Ialysos also issued coins on the Phoenician standard, depicting the head of an eagle and a winged boar.

The downfall of Lindos began in the early fifth century B.C. when the Persians made their appearance in the Aegean. Persian intrusion resulted in the conquest of the island and in the loss of the prized Lindian fleet. Robbed of power, Lindos could no longer lead

The little bay, Mikros Ialos or St. Paul's, south of the acropolis in Lindos

From the height of the acropolis to the shimmering sea below

The large bay, Megalos Ialos, north of the acropolis at Lindos

View of the big bay from the acropolis

in Rhodes. The aristocratic families of Ialysos, who had been dependent primarily on an agricultural economy, survived the Persian invasion and assumed greater power.

The excavations on the acropolis of Lindos were initiated by the Danish archaeologists Finch and Blinkenberg and the restoration work was done by the Italians. The Danish findings are catalogued in a collection of six volumes. The first four books, written by Blinkenberg, describe the objects and the inscriptions that were found. Two later volumes on the architecture were published by Dyggve, another Danish archaeologist, who disputed many of his predecessors' theories.

A marble stele was found with a precious inscription known as the Temple Chronicle. It recounts the history of the temple and includes an impressive list of offerings through the years. It was composed in the first century B.C. and is now in the Copenhagen Museum. The Chronicle reported, among other things, that the original statue of Athena was affixed to the short wall of the cella of the temple and welcomed worshippers as they entered. The statue may have been too bulky or too unbalanced to stand alone.

From around 1912 through 1948 Rhodes was an Italian dependency and the Italian style and influence are still felt today. The Italian archaeologists Maiuri and Jacopi worked on the Lindos site and are credited with the restoration of antiquities on the acropolis and with the current appearance of the towering site.

The acropolis is reached by passing through Lindos, a quaint town of flat-roofed homes with blazing whitewashed walls and narrow streets paved with clean smooth sea-pebbles. Visitors pass fortified medieval walls and a steep staircase leading to the palace of the Governor. An exedra carved out of rock was found on a plateau at the foot of the staircase. A relief emerges from the exedra and depicts the stern of an ancient trireme. The trireme served as the base of an admiral's statue carved by Pythokritos at the beginning of the second century B.C. Pythocritos also carved the ineffable Nike of Samothrace, excibited in the Louvre. She was on the prow of a ship leaning into the wind about to take flight. The wind molded a sheer,

The castle and an ancient column from Doric stoa

beautifully composed fabric against her form and the sculptor masterfully worked the marble to suggest a loose wind-swept opalescent dress.

Remains of an ancient staircase are still in situ; it is believed to be the original entrance to the acropolis. A medieval Government House and the remains of the Byzantine Church of St. John from the thirteenth century A.D. are also in place.

The formal staircase ascended to a large Doric stoa adjacent to the propylaia. The elegant stoa, built around 200 B.C., faced north toward the temple. Originally it had about forty-two columns. Twenty have survived and are still standing. The eight central columns faced the staircase to the propylaia and enhanced the temple approach. The only trace of the propylaia is its tenacious foundation.

The ruins of an ancient Lindian theatre dating from the fourth century B.C. have been excavated on the western slope of the acropolis. The theatre had been sliced from the steep rockface and had an unparalleled view of the sea. Fragments of the twenty-six semicircular rows of seats have survived.

The Knights of Rhodes transformed the Castle at Lindos into a fortress. It is now forsaken but for the decaying echoes of its ponderous past. It was last used in the midnineteenth century by the Turks as a garrison. Even though it was virtually immune from attack because of the precipitous bluff from which it emerged, the Knights nevertheless sealed the perimeter walls and made it irrefutably unconquerable. The impregnable walls give the fortress a strong warlike appearance in marked contrast to the elegant beauty of the stately Greek temple.

On the northern slope of the acropolis there is a small shrine from the tenth to ninth centuries B.C. where bulls were sacrificed. It was called the Boukopion. The ancient references to sacrifices to the Lindian Athena were bloodless although some evidence of animal sacrifice has been found within the temple itself. It was initially believed that the Boukopion was intended to keep the temple pure and uncontaminated. However, in light of the discovery of animal

Semi-circular exedra

Byzantine church of St. John

Majestic view from the castle that revealed all enemy approaches

Ancient excavated ruins

Restorative work on the temple of the Lindian Athena

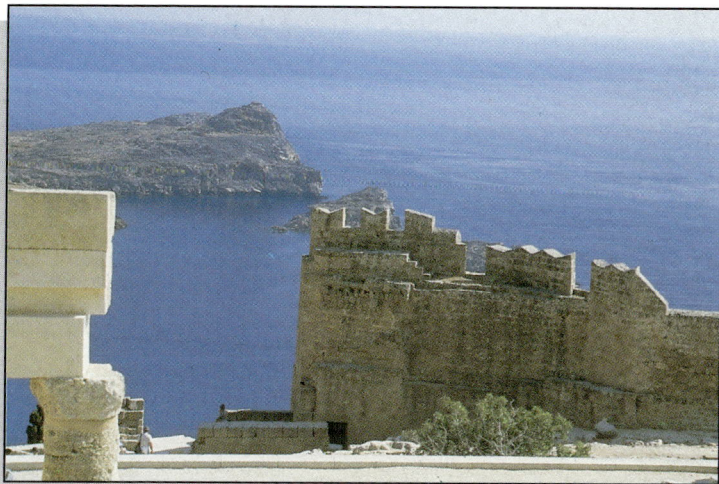

Incomparable view of the sea from atop the acropolis

Restorative work currently ongoing on acropolis

Site from atop the acropolis

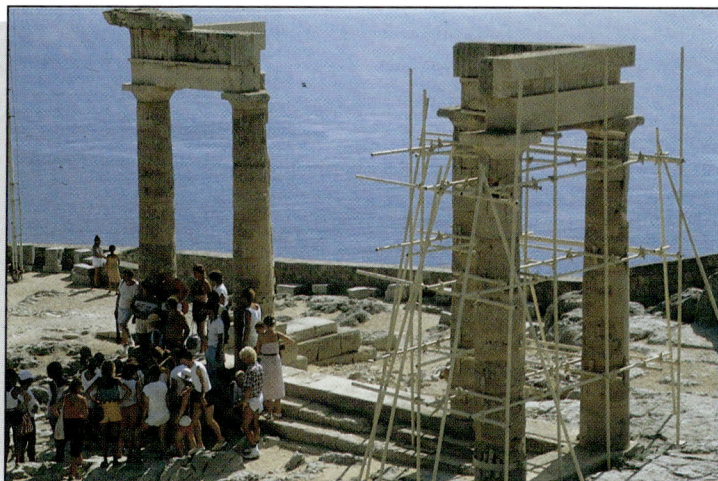

Foreign tourists flock to the site of the Lindian Athena

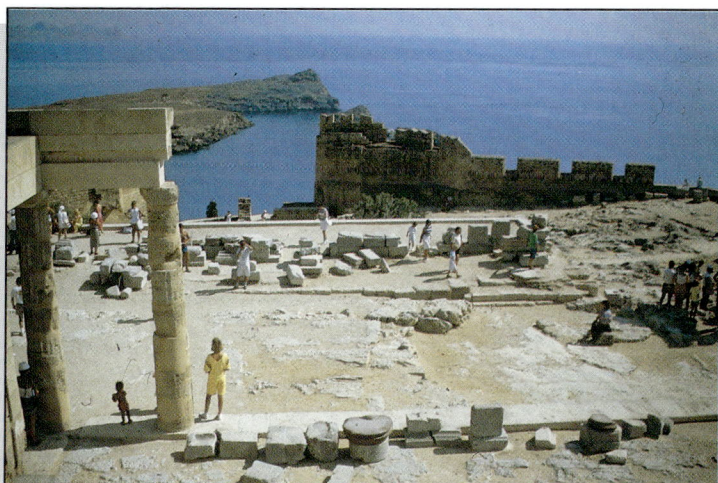

View from the temple showing the perimeter of the castle and the bay

bones and other evidence of sacrifice in the temple itself, it is not entirely clear if indeed the temple was untainted by slaughter.

The modern village of Lindos, about one-quarter the size of ancient Lindos, is situated at the base of the acropolis. From the sixth to the tenth centuries A.D. the population of the town diminished drastically. In the eleventh century, however, new churches were built signifying that the population began to grow again. In the fifteenth and sixteenth centuries Lindos prospered again because of the sea. This success is reflected in the style and the size of the private homes of the period. Many seventeenth century Lindian homes are in a good state of preservation. The oldest is inscribed with the date 1599.

The most impressive old stone homes are those that belonged to the venturesome sea captains. The facade facing the street was protected by a characteristic high wall and the main entrance led to an expansive central courtyard. Carvings in relief border the windows and doors. The carvings depict birds or floral designs or a cable or rope pattern. The number of cables used as surrounds represented the number of ships owned by the captain. The floors were often pebbled in a smooth black and white mosaic pattern.

Lindian pottery, plates in particular, is of some renown. It first appeared in the sixteenth century A.D. The popular myth is that the Knights captured a boat carrying Persian artisans and held them captive on Rhodes where they were forced to teach their craft. There is a discernible eastern influence in the designs. They are brightly colored vegetation motifs in shades of red and blue. Each plate was pierced with two holes for hanging. This custom traces back to about 700 B.C. when plates from Kamiros were found pierced with holes in just the same way. A collection of Lindian plates is exhibited in Athens at the Benaki Museum.

The beauty of Rhodes has inspired seamen and poets, scholars and kings. For Lawrence Durrell it has a haunting enduring power that he captured in the Epilogue to *Reflections on a Marine Venus*. He may have expressed the collective yearning of all who see and discover this bewitching place. He too was mesmerized by the

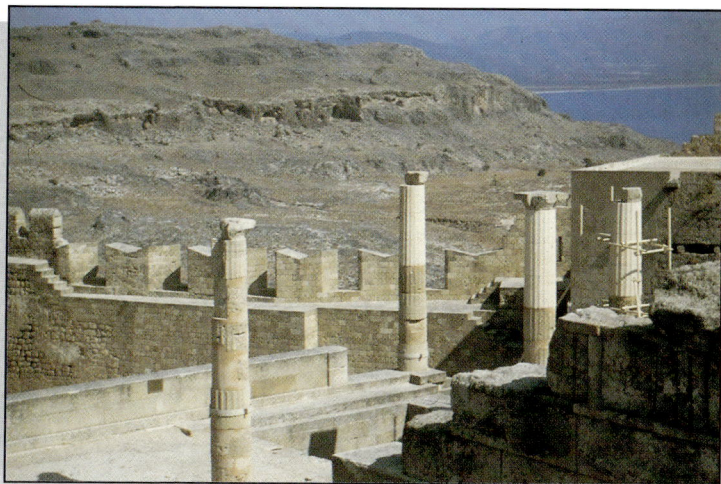

Stunning mixture of the medieval and the ancient surrounding the castle.

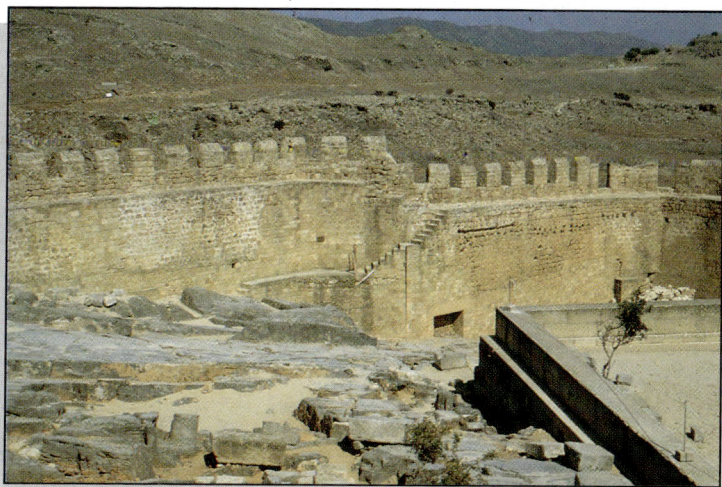

The fortified walls of the medieval castle

strains of her lingering beckoning song:

> "The Sporades are lean wolves and hunt in packs; waterless, eroded by the sun. They branch off on every side as you coast along the shores of Anatolia. Then towards afternoon the shaggy green of Cos comes up; and then, slithering out of the wintry blue the moist green flanks of Rhodes.
>
> It is good to see places where one has been happy in the past - to see them after many years and in different circumstances. The child is asleep in its rugs: that long, much-loved, much travelled coastline breasts its way up against the liner's deck until the town fans out - each minaret like the loved worn face of an earthly friend. I am looking, as if into a well, to recapture the faces of Hoyle, Gideon, Mills - and the dark vehement grace of E.
>
> Ahead of us the night gathers, a different night, and Rhodes begins to fall into the unresponding sea from which only memory can rescue it. The clouds hang high over Anatolia. Other islands? Other futures?
>
> Not, I think, after one has lived with the Marine Venus. The wound she gives one must carry to the world's end."